Discourse and Language Learning: A Relational Approach to Syllabus Design

Discourse and Language Learning: A Relational Approach to Syllabus Design

Winifred Crombie

Oxford University Press
1985

91-105

Oxford University Press
Walton Street, Oxford OX2 6DP

Oxford London New York Toronto Melbourne Auckland
Kuala Lumpur Singapore Hong Kong Tokyo Delhi
Bombay Madras Calcutta Karachi Nairobi
Dar es Salaam Cape Town

and associated companies in
Beirut Berlin Ibadan Mexico City Nicosia

OXFORD is a trade mark of Oxford University Press

ISBN 0 19 437070 4

Typeset in Linotron 202 by
Graphicraft Typesetters Ltd. Hong Kong
Printed in Hong Kong

Acknowledgements

Acknowledgements are made to the following for their permission to reproduce the following copyright material

BBC, for the extract from a BBC Radio 4 programme, 'Tuesday Call', broadcast on 9 November 1982.

Boots The Chemists Ltd for part of the text of their advertisement used in 1975.

Hertfordshire Mercury, for the report on 'Hertfordshire Yesterdays', from the Hertfordshire Mercury 15 October 1982.

IPC Magazines Ltd. 1982, for the passage from 'Woman' magazine on 'Dustpic'.

Nature Magazine, for 'Molecular Structure of Nucleic Acids: A Structure for Deoxyribose Nucleic Acid' by Watson & Crick, published in Nature, 25 April 1953.

Observer, for the advertisement 'High Technology U.K. Company', 18 September 1982.

Production Engineer, for 'Using computers in manufacturing', which appeared in Production Engineer November 1978.

The Times Higher Education Supplement, for 'Devon Faces Y.T.S. Cash Crisis', THES 23 September 1983.

Contents

Introduction

Over the past few years, I have detected a growing feeling of unease about the content and implications of research in the area of 'communicative' syllabus design. I have discussed this with many postgraduate linguistics students who are, or have been, directly involved in language teaching and course design. In these discussions, four issues which I believe to be extremely important have repeatedly been raised. First, there is a feeling that the significance which has rightly been accorded to function has led to a tendency to neglect, or even deny, the equivalent importance of structure. Secondly, it is felt that research has been too firmly centred on English for Specific Purposes and that the issues involved in designing general syllabuses have been neglected. Thirdly, it has been suggested that discussions about syllabus design are sometimes conducted at a level of complexity, abstraction, and idealization which seems not only inappropriate to the real problem which has to be tackled, but which also threatens to create a positive barrier to more constructive and productive discussion. I believe that this may be the unfortunate consequence of the fact that many linguists, perhaps particularly those linguists who are concerned with applications, are often deeply committed to the belief that it is of fundamental importance that they should bear in mind at all times, and within whatever context they are writing, the need to attempt to influence the future direction of their subject. Fourthly, there is a widespread belief that too many parameters have been introduced into the discussion of syllabus design, many of which involve 'red herrings' in the form of categories which are impossible to deal with in any systematic way — categories which syllabus designers are somehow expected to take account of but about which linguists have, at least at present, very little that is of practical help to say. Taken together, these four issues seem to be leading to a belief that linguistics, except in so far as it can help to refine and improve structural categories, has little to offer the syllabus designer, particularly the syllabus designer who is involved in the construction of syllabuses for general use. This, combined with the fact that there is an increasing interest among linguists and educationalists in methodological matters and a reduction of interest in matters relating to syllabus design, could lead to a position in which discussion of some of the interesting questions that have been raised in the last decade is stifled.

This book is written in response to this problem and, in particular, in response to the four issues which seem to me to have given rise to it. The approach to syllabus design adopted here is based on four simple premises:

1 that structure and function are equally important;
2 that discussions about syllabus design should begin with a consideration of the principles involved in designing general syllabuses rather than with a consideration of needs specification for learners who may have specific communicative objectives;
3 that syllabus designers must necessarily restrict themselves to categories that are finite, systematizable, and at least reasonably well understood;
4 that syllabus designers should take as their starting point and organizational principle those aspects of discourse construction and comprehension which all learners, whatever their cultural and language background, have in common.

The discussion centres on various types and categories of relationship between discourse units and it is suggested that these relationships — which underlie the construction of coherent discourse — can provide us with a conceptual framework for our syllabus, into which we can insert, in a systematic way, those constructions and lexical items which we wish to introduce at various stages.

This book is intended largely as an introduction to a new approach to syllabus design. It may not, on its own, supply sufficient descriptive detail for anyone wishing to design a syllabus on the basis of the principles outlined. However, I have written a companion volume, *Process and relation in discourse and language learning*, which provides more detailed guidance.

The approach outlined here is a development of my entry for the 1980 English Language Competition run by the English-Speaking Union. I should like to thank the organizers and judges of that competition for providing the impetus for the initial formulation of the ideas on which this work is based. For their contribution towards the development of these ideas, I wish to think both my students and my colleagues in the linguistics group at The Hatfield Polytechnic. Thanks are also due to those at The Hatfield Polytechnic who are responsible for having made available to me the facilities and resources necessary for the undertaking of this work and for granting me sabbatical leave, without which it would have been extremely difficult to bring the work to completion. Finally, while not wishing to suggest that he would necessarily agree with my conclusions, I am particularly grateful to Professor Henry Widdowson for the help and encouragement that he has given me throughout the writing of this book.

1 Approaches to language syllabus design

A whole is not the sum of its parts (if by 'parts' we mean only the isolated segments), but only of its parts plus their relationships.

Becker, *A tagmemic approach to paragraph analysis*

Still, in spite of their capital importance, it is better to approach the problem of units through the study of value, for in my opinion value is of prime importance.

Saussure, *Course in general linguistics*

A great deal has been said and written over the centuries about language learning. In the last twenty years or so, much of the discussion and debate has centred on the issue of how best to design language syllabuses. And yet, for all that has been said and written, only one approach to syllabus design has so far been given serious consideration: an approach which selects language units for progressive assimilation by learners. Whether these units are selected primarily according to morphological and syntactic considerations (the *structural syllabus*), or whether they are grouped according to criteria which are primarily semantic and are not strictly ordered and graded (the *notional syllabus*), the situation remains basically the same: what we are being offered is essentially, if not wholly, an inventory of discrete units (Widdowson 1979: 247–250). What we have not been offered so far is an approach to syllabus design which takes adequate account of language as coherent discourse — which gives adequate recognition to language as dynamic interaction governed by co-operative principles according to which participants in a discourse give different values to the same linguistic units in relation to the linguistic context (co-text), and the general situational context in which they occur. In different contexts, the declarative 'I'm terribly hot' may, for example, function as a command to act (to open a door or a window, for example), as a question (requesting/requiring a reason for the heat), as an item of information, as a warning, a threat, an insult. It may be an expression of surprise, of pleasure, of displeasure. It may be ironic. It could be a reason for something or a result of something. In both 1 and 2, 'I'm terribly hot' is a response giving information. In 2, however, it has the additional discourse value, *reason*:

1 A: How do you feel?
   B: I'm terribly hot.
2 A: Why did you take off your jacket?
   B: I'm terribly hot.

If we wish to design language syllabuses which will encourage course writers to concentrate not only on isolated linguistic units, but on coherent spoken and written discourse, then the concept of discourse value must in some sense be central. Discourse value is an inherently relational concept. Linguistic units do not have values in isolation. They assume particular values through their relationship with co-text and situational context.

The reason why syllabus designers have in the past concentrated on linguistic units in isolation rather than on the relationships between linguistic units in context and, hence, on the establishment of discourse values, is not hard to find. In spite of the efforts of speech act theorists, attempts to identify discourse values (or speech acts) have not met with a great deal of success (Levinson 1983: 226–278). Indeed, some linguists, particularly those working in the area of the ethnography of speaking (e.g. Bauman and Sherzer 1974), are reluctantly accepting Wittgenstein's view (1958:10–11) that there are as many discourse values (or speech acts) as there are roles in the indefinite variety of language games (or speech events) that human beings are capable of inventing. Nevertheless, the situation as far as language syllabus design is concerned is far from hopeless. There is no need to give up the attempt to design language syllabuses which will be truly communicative (in the sense that they will truly encourage the development of language courses where there is a concentration on the creation and interpretation of coherent discourse in which linguistic units assume values by virtue of their contextual relationships). It is important, however, if our attempts are to succeed, to begin such a task from as solid a linguistic base as possible and to concentrate initially on those discourse values about which linguists do have a great deal to say, much of which could be directly relevant to the design of language syllabuses. Those values are the ones which I shall refer to as binary values.

Discourse values may be divided into two types: *unitary values* and *binary values.* I believe that binary discourse values (e.g. Reason — Result; Condition — Consequence), are the obvious starting point for an attempt to design language syllabuses which concentrate on discourse. There appear to be a limited and analytically manageable number of binary values and these have a high degree of comparability across languages (Longacre 1972: 52). Additionally, since binary values are very often lexically and syntactically signalled, the study of binary values has direct implications for the study of vocabulary and syntax.

My main concern in this book will be with the ways in which binary values are established through contextual relationships and, in particular, with the various words and expressions in English which signal such relationships and which are the basis of the actual linguistic realization of these active contextual meanings. I shall suggest that the identification of such binary values provides us with an important clue to the ways in which we might design language syllabuses concentrating on the relationships within discourse which give meaning to linguistic units and, additionally, that the recognition of binary discourse values is likely to prove directly relevant to the understanding of unitary discourse values.

Unitary discourse values and binary discourse values

The *discourse value* of an utterance is its *significance* or *communicative function* within a discourse as distinct from its *sentence meaning* (or *conceptual content*). *Sentence meaning* is determined largely with respect to the interaction between words and the structures in which they occur; *discourse value* is determined largely with respect to the interaction between sentence meaning and context. The sentence meaning of 'He broke his leg' in 3 and 4 is the same. In 3, however, it has the discourse value — *reason*, whereas in 4 it has the discourse value — *result*:

3 A: Why did he have to go into hospital?
  B: He broke his leg.
4 A: What was the result of the car crash?
  B: He broke his leg.

In dealing with discourse values, we are dealing with language in use, with the meanings that attach to units of language by virtue of the co-text and situational context in which they occur.

I referred above to the fact that discourse values can be divided into two main types: *unitary values* and *binary values*. The term *binary value* is used to refer to the significance which attaches to units of language within a spoken or written discourse by virtue of the specific type of relationship which they bear to one another. Thus, binary values have two parts (or members): they require for their realization two related propositions or groups of propositions. For example, the term *Reason — Result* and the term *Condition — Consequence* may be used as labels for specific types of binary value. You cannot simply have a reason, you must have a *reason for* something: you cannot simply have a result, you must have a *result of* something. Likewise, you cannot simply have a condition, you must have a *condition of* or a *condition for* something: you cannot simply have a consequence, you must have a *consequence of* something. The relationship between the two clauses in 5 is that of Reason — Result; the relationship between the two clauses in 6 is that of Condition — Consequence:

5 Because you were late, I missed the bus.
      (Reason)   (Result)
6 If you're late, I'll miss the bus.
    (Condition)   (Consequence)

Binary values may themselves be divided into two types which I shall refer to as *interactional values* and *general discoursal values*. The term *interactional value* is used to refer to the functional components of a conversational discourse and generally relates to the interaction between the conversational contributions of different speakers. Thus, for example, the interactional relationship between A and B in 7 is that of Elicitation — Reply (Sinclair and Coulthard 1975), or, broadly, Question and Answer:

7 A: Why did he do it?   (Elicitation)
   B: He needed the money. (Reply)

The term *general discoursal value* is used to refer to values of a type which can occur in any type of discourse, including conversational discourse. Reason — Result (or Result — Reason) is a general discoursal value. It is exemplified both in 7, where the *result* is ['he did it'] and the *reason* is 'he needed the money', and in 8:

8 The king decided to levy taxes (result), because he needed the money (reason).

So far, I have, for the sake of simplicity, referred to binary values as those values which exist only where two members (or units of language which are related in a specific way) are present. However, a distinction should be made between those values which are *inherently binary* and those which are *presumptively binary*. Thus, for example, as I mentioned earlier, you cannot simply have a result, you must have a *result of* something. In order for a unit of discourse to have attached to it the value *result*, there must be present another unit of discourse to which is attached the value *reason* (see examples 3, 4, 5, 7 and 8 above). Thus, *reason* and *result* are inherently binary. However, if we look again at interactional values, we can see that some are *inherently binary* — that is, they can exist only as one member of a pair and are defined with respect to that pairing — whereas some are *presumptively binary* — that is, they create the expectation that a unit of language with a specific type of value will follow: they do not require the existence of such a unit in order that their own value be established. Thus, for example, *reply* is an inherently binary value: you cannot simply have a reply, you must have a *reply to* something. The value *elicitation* is, however, only presumptively binary: an elicitation expects, but does not require a reply.

Although I shall be concentrating in this book on binary values, I shall from time to time make reference to unitary values. Segments of language within a discourse which have unitary values (e.g. *warning, threat, insult*) do not presuppose that there will be other segments to which they will be related in specific, definable ways: they may enter into a whole range of different relationships with other segments within the co-text.

The signalling of binary discourse values

Every language has a large number of words and expressions part of whose function is to make explicit the semantic relationships between units in a discourse. These words and expressions act as signals of those relationships between units which are the basis of the realization of active contextual meanings (Winter 1977). For example, each of the English words in the following list is *value indicative*: *although, because, concede, concession, conclude, conclusion, converse, conversely, deny, denial, nevertheless, purpose, reason, so, therefore*, etc. Words and expressions of this type are semantically important in that they act as signals of discourse value. They are also syntactically important in terms of the types of linkage that they make between propositions. Some of these words and expressions are subordinators, some are not. In each of the examples 9–11, the Reason — Result (or Result — Reason) relationship is signalled in a different way:

9 Because I missed the train, I'm going to be late for work.
10 I missed the train so I'm going to be late for work.
11 I'm going to be late for work. The reason is that I missed the train.

Thus, these words and expressions not only signal the discourse value of a unit, but also its focus or weighting within the discourse. Within the discourse as a whole, the syntactic properties of these value signals is clearly of stylistic importance. The fact that words such as *because* simultaneously signal unit value (i.e. reason) and unit weighting (i.e. subordinate) is a helpful clue to the way in which we might design language syllabuses that attach equal importance to the semantic and syntactic aspects of linguistic communication.

Since binary values are established through relationships between units within a discourse, the signalling of relationship is simultaneously a signalling of value. Relationships may be signalled in a number of different ways. In spoken discourse, intonation may provide clues to relational values (see Crombie 1985). However, binary values are not always explicitly signalled. In 9–11 above, Reason — Result was signalled by *because, so* and *reason*. In 12, however, although it appears that the relationship between the two sentences is that of Reason — Result, there is no explicit lexico-syntactic signalling. Where such a sequence occurs, particularly where such a sequence occurs in written discourse, value assignment will be made with reference to wider context:

12 I missed the train. I'm going to be late for work.

For the language learner, adequate control of the value signalling systems of his target language is a vital element in the development of communicative competence. For the language teacher and syllabus designer, the introduction into teaching programmes of the value signalling systems of the target language provides a framework for the introduction of the learner to language as a communicative dynamic and for a movement towards unsignalled values and unfamiliar value assignments. The ultimate aim is that the learner should reach a degree of competence at which he can not only recognize and use value signals, but also recognize where and when they need not be introduced and where and when they must not be.

The *signalling* of binary values should not be confused with the *labelling* of unitary values. Values which are inherently binary are established through relationship between units of language within a discourse. Thus, in examples 9, 10 and 11 above, the two clauses are involved in the relationship of Reason — Result. Furthermore, binary values are often explicitly signalled within a discourse. Where they are, it is possible to abstract the linguistic units which realize them from the environment in which these units occur and still be able to identify them. Thus, we do not need to know anything about the situation in which 13 is used in order to know that 'I like doing that sort of thing' is being offered as a *reason* and 'I kicked the cat' as a *result*:

13 I kicked the cat because I like doing that sort of thing.

You might not be inclined to accept that 'I like doing that sort of thing' is an *adequate* or *sufficient* reason for kicking the cat, but you cannot deny that it is being offered as a reason.

In the case of unitary values, the situation is different. Unitary values are not established through a direct relationship between two specific units within a discourse. They are very rarely identified linguistically within a discourse and they are almost always tied inescapably to a specific context of situation. Thus, although we can identify the fact that the two clauses below have the binary value Condition — Consequence, we cannot say, in the absence of a knowledge of the specific situation in which they are uttered, whether they are, taken together, to be identified as having the unitary value, *threat*, or the unitary value, *incentive*, or, indeed, neither of these:

14 If you do that again, I'll read you another story.

Depending on the context in which it occurs, 15 could have almost any unitary value. In many contexts, it would have the value, *compliment*; in others, it would have the value, *insult*:

15 You are a very attractive woman.

At first sight, it might appear that the occurrence of the word *suggest* in 16 identifies the unitary value, *suggestion*:

16 I suggest that you do that exercise again.

In fact, as every native speaker of English knows, in certain situations, it would be intended not as a suggestion but as an *order*. Indeed; instances such as 17 are very common:

17 I suggest that you do that exercise again — and that's an order.

One important point to note about 17 is that the word *order* does, in fact, identify the speaker's intentions in relation to the unitary value of the first clause. Examples of this type are rare. It is only very occasionally that a speaker will retrospectively (see example 17) or prospectively specify his intentions in this way. Where he does do so, it is generally because he either wishes to reinforce a particular unitary value or believes that the context may be misleading or inadequate for the establishment of that value.

For a time, some philosophers took the view, expressed initially by Austin (1962), that there were certain types of utterance, called performatives, with which particular unitary values were inevitably associated. Thus, it was argued that utterances like 18 inevitably had the unitary value, *promise*, and like 19 inevitably had the unitary value, *bet*:

18 I promise to pay John the ransom money.
19 I bet John £5.

However, there are contexts in which this is not the case. B's utterance in 20 is not a promise, neither is B's utterance in 21 a bet:

20 A: Now think. What do you do if he has a hostage?
   B: I promise to pay John the ransom money.
21 A: Now think. What do you do if the race is on?
   B: I bet John £5.

I shall be arguing throughout this book for an approach to language syllabus design where the relationships between units of discourse which establish those active contextual meanings that I have referred to as binary values is given centrality — for an approach which focuses on the creation and understanding of coherent discourse and which, therefore, moves beyond the idea of a syllabus as being constituted necessarily of an inventory of discrete units only. I believe that a syllabus can, and perhaps should, be conceived of, at least in part, as a series of what I shall refer to as *relational frames*, that is, as a series of frameworks, each of which is made up of a group indicating the various discoursal relationships between units which are to be given prominence (see the final section of this chapter, and Chapter 5). However, I shall certainly not be arguing for an approach which abandons all of the important lessons which can be learned from the debate on syllabus design which has taken place particularly in the last twenty years. The approach adopted in this book grows directly out of that debate and I shall, therefore, provide a short discussion of the *structural* and *notional* approaches to the design of language syllabuses before providing an outline of my own approach in the final section of this chapter. Before doing either of these, however, I shall discuss briefly the terms *syllabus*, *materials*, and *methodology*.

The terms 'syllabus', 'materials', and 'methodology'

If we are to understand clearly what we mean when we refer to syllabus design, it is necessary to clarify what is generally meant by the term 'syllabus' itself in the context of language teaching. A syllabus, as generally conceived, is a list or inventory of items or units with which learners are to be familiarized. Language learners are unlikely to come into direct contact with syllabuses. What they will come into direct contact with are the course materials which are employed in the implementation of a syllabus. They may, however, if they use a coursebook in which learning units are labelled or glossed by some of the elements which constitute the syllabus itself, come into contact in this way with a modified and abbreviated version of the syllabus. Thus, we must make a distinction between a *syllabus* and the *materials* used in the implementation of that syllabus. We must make a further distinction between the materials used in implementing a syllabus and the *methodologies* employed in selecting and exploiting these materials. How you choose materials and how you decide to use them (what you decide to do with them) is a matter of methodology.

Thus, a language learner cannot be motivated directly by a syllabus. Nevertheless, the way in which a syllabus is designed may motivate a learner indirectly by encouraging the use of particular types of materials and particular methodologies. Whilst a syllabus designer may not be in a position to *dictate* the materials and methodologies which will be used in the implementation of his syllabus — unless, of course, he implements it himself — he should be in a position to *suggest* that particular methodologies and, hence, particular types of materials, might be appropriate to its implementation. Thus, although this book is concerned primarily with syllabus design, I shall from time to time make reference to materials and methodology. I do not believe that the design of a syllabus can or should be seen as a quite separate issue from its implementation. Indeed, it seems to me to be important that syllabus designers should be prepared at the very least to provide a rationale for the design of a syllabus which is sufficiently explicit to ensure that course writers will be in a position to make judgements about the type of materials that will be appropriate to its implementation, and about the methodologies that might suitably be used in exploiting these materials.

The language syllabus: structural and notional–functional approaches

Increasingly, syllabus designers seem to be adopting the view that the best syllabus will, in many cases, be one which is based on eclecticism: one which emerges from a combination of approaches rather than from a single approach (see, for example, Bell 1981: 56; Wilkins 1974). Nevertheless, it is important to make a distinction between the two main approaches to syllabus design — the *structural approach* and the *notional–functional approach* (sometimes referred to simply as the *notional approach*) — which provide the input to such syllabuses, and to recognize that these approaches have not always been seen as complementary (Wilkins 1976), and, indeed, need not now necessarily be seen as complementary.

In order to make a useful comparison between the structural and notional–functional approaches to syllabus design, it will be necessary to refer again to the distinction made earlier in this chapter between *sentence meaning* (i.e. conceptual content) and *discourse value* (i.e. significance or communicative function). A linguistic unit which has a particular meaning may function differently in different contexts and will, therefore, have different discourse values in different contexts. The proponents of structural syllabuses have never claimed that discourse values are taken into account directly within their syllabuses. The proponents of notional–functional syllabuses, on the other hand, have made such a claim (Wilkins 1976). Before attempting to determine whether or not notional–functional syllabuses could in fact take account of discourse values (or functions), it will be necessary to examine in a little detail the assumptions which underlie structural and notional –functional approaches to syllabus design.

Every syllabus constructed according to structural principles has as part of its inventory a list of linguistic units which are formally (or structurally) labelled. In general terms, a structural syllabus might be described as an inventory of labelled items and units to which learners are to be progressively introduced, the units being labelled and grouped largely in terms of their formal properties and ordered and graded according to a number of linguistic and pedagogic criteria. This description is, however, an oversimplification, and some of the criticisms that have been made of structural syllabuses (e.g. Wilkins 1976), seem to result directly from this type of oversimplification.

It has been claimed that structural syllabuses are inherently insensitive to meaning — that their categories are grammatical rather than semantico-grammatical — and that their linear, hierarchical organization is ill-adapted to the exploitation of the meaning potentials inherent in structures. Whereas both of these criticisms may be justified in the case of some structural syllabuses, they are certainly not equally justified in the case of all structural syllabuses.

Structural syllabuses need not be, and in practice rarely are, strictly linear. They need not, and in practice rarely do, neglect the meaning potentials of structures. Structural syllabuses are often cyclic: the same construction may be introduced several times at different places in the syllabuses, each time associated with the realization of a specific, structure-related meaning. Thus, for example, the Present Simple in English may be introduced several times, each time associated with different adverbials (e.g. *every day/often*; *tomorrow/next week*), which provide the co-text which realizes a different meaning potential (e.g. habitual/futural) of the construction. Furthermore, structural syllabuses almost always have a number of learning units which are devoted either to contrasting different meaning potentials of the same construction, or contrasting different constructions (e.g. Past Simple and Present Perfect in English), in defined contexts which highlight differences in meaning.

At this point, it is useful to bear in mind the distinction between a syllabus and its implementation, that is, between a syllabus and the materials and methodologies used to exploit that syllabus (see the third section of this chapter). Many of the course materials and methodologies that have traditionally been associated with the implementation of structural syllabuses seem often to have been selected specifically because of their value in drawing attention to both meaning and discourse value. Indeed, many — if not most — of the questions associated with reading and listening comprehension exercises seem designed, although probably not always with the same degree of awareness, in such a way as to compensate for what could be seen as certain syllabus deficiencies by drawing attention in a detailed way to meaning and discourse value (e.g. 'What did she *suggest*?'; 'What did she do *next*?'; '*Why* did she do it?'; 'Had she *already left* when he *arrived*?'). Certainly, too many of these exercises merely involve passive recognition. Nevertheless, they do seem to play an important role in the development of communicative competence.

It would appear, then, that some of the criticisms that have been levelled against structural syllabuses are *wholly* justified only in relation to badly designed structural syllabuses. Furthermore, the determination to separate the discussion of syllabus design from the discussion of course content and methodology has meant that critics, whilst claiming that structural syllabuses fail to encourage the development of communicative competence, have often neglected to note that the language courses which implement these structural syllabuses often make up for some of the deficiencies inherent in the syllabus itself. This, of course, is not irrelevant. Whatever the primary focus of our interest in language learning, our concern must ultimately be with courses as a whole. Whilst I would not deny that many of the adverse criticisms of structural syllabuses are justified, I believe that many of them are *wholly* justified only in the case of badly designed and carelessly implemented structural syllabuses.

The concept of the notional–functional syllabus emerged from Council of Europe research and was originally associated largely with Wilkins (1972a & b, 1973, 1974, 1976) and Van Ek (1975). The crucial question that must be asked in relation to this concept is whether it is capable of realization. Could such a thing as a notional–functional syllabus actually be constructed and, if so, would it be essentially different from a structural syllabus?

Theoretically, a notional–functional syllabus might be described as a list of *notional* (or semantic) labels and a list of *functional* (or discourse value) labels. However, it is doubtful whether such a list could be regarded as a syllabus at all since it would, as we shall see, provide course writers with very little guidance. In practice, what is often referred to as a notional–functional syllabus is a list of linguistic units to each of which is attached a semantic and/or discourse value label.

Leaving aside lexical items, the categories with which we would be concerned in attempting to construct a notional–functional syllabus can be roughly divided into two types: *semantico-grammatical categories* and *categories of communicative function* (Wilkins 1979b). The first of these might be defined as a category designed to cope with the interrelationship between form and meaning; the second, as a category designed to cope with discourse values. I shall discuss each of these categories in turn.

As far as semantico-grammatical categories are concerned, the only difference in the end between a structural syllabus and a notional–functional syllabus seems to be a difference in emphasis. Although the proponents of notional–functional syllabuses avoid ordered exposure to the grammar of language (Wilkins 1976: 19), and sometimes claim that the introduction of grammar is a matter of methodology (Wilkins 1976: 14), in practice, they must, directly or indirectly, make reference to certain formal items. If they do not do so, they have not provided a syllabus at all but rather, some guidelines for the construction of a syllabus. There is very little that a course writer can do with a list of *notions* such as *location*, *place*, *motion*. One thing that he can do, however, is to list under each of these headings certain prepositions, adverbs etc. which may realize these notions in context and decide which of these he will include in his course and where. If he does do this, he has effectively written part of the syllabus himself.

Theoretically, the main difference between a structural syllabus and a notional–functional syllabus is that, in the latter case, categories of communicative function are included. However, categories of communicative function are designed to cope with discourse values and, as we have seen (in the first two sections of this chapter), units of language do not have values in isolation. They assume particular values through their relationship with co-text and situational context. Almost any unit of language can have almost any discourse value. This being the case, it is almost impossible to imagine what actual use a list of discourse values, such as *compliment*, *insult*, *threat*, *warning*, *suggestion*, could be to a course writer. In effect, the only thing that he can do once again is to write part of the syllabus himself. This time, however, his task is almost impossible. If almost any unit of language can have almost any value, how is he to decide what to include and where? In fact, there are two possible courses open to him. One thing that he can do is to list under each of the values with which he has been supplied, any semi-idiomatic expressions which may be associated with it. A semi-idiomatic expression is an expression whose discourse value is *relatively* fixed. Thus, under the heading of *suggestion*, he might have a list of grammatical expressions including *Shall [we]...*, *Let's ...* and *Why don't [we] ....* There are two dangers here. First, the real problem — that almost any unit of language can have almost any discourse value — has effectively been ignored. Secondly, the expressions which have been listed are

not idioms, they are *semi*-idioms. Their value is not fixed, it is
relatively fixed. It is perfectly possible to envisage situations in
which these grammatical expressions would function not as *suggestions*, but as, for example, *directives* or *elicitations*. What the
course writer (now also syllabus designer) is in danger of doing here
is creating a positive barrier to the development of communicative
competence in learners by encouraging the assumption that, in their
target language at least, value, like meaning, is more or less fixed —
that discourse value is a property of a particular grammatical
expression rather than of the relationship between units of language and the linguistic and non-linguistic context in which they
occur. In order to avoid this problem, the course writer, faced with
the same list of discourse values, might take the only other route
open to him, which is to ignore entirely the fact that he has, at best,
only part of a syllabus, and decide simply to create or collect course
materials (dialogues, stories etc.) in which several — or many — of
the linguistic units which occur actually do, by virtue of the
contexts in which they occur, have the specified discourse values. If
he decides to concentrate on each of the specified discourse values
in turn — rather than on several together — he will probably create
rather than collect most of his course materials. It is unlikely to be
any easier to find relatively short stretches of language in which a
significant number of different units have the same discourse value,
than it is to find relatively short stretches of language in which the
same construction occurs a significant number of times. In addition
to creating and/or collecting course materials of this type, the
course writer can design exercises, including controlled participation exercises (Bell 1981: 44 and 45), where learners are presented
with contexts in which it is likely that they will create linguistic
units associated with the specified value or values. Unless, however,
he decides to have no additional controls on the language which
occurs in his learning units, the course writer will have to make
decisions on the basis of other criteria — probably the same sort of
criteria that are associated with a structural syllabus — about what
to include and where. If he makes decisions on the basis of the same
sort of criteria that are applied in the design of structural syllabuses,
then he will, in effect, be designing for himself part of another type
of syllabus — the structural syllabus. If he avoids making any
decisions of this type altogether, then he will effectively have made
a decision of another type: he will have decided that materials
and methodology can somehow be a substitute for a syllabus.
The outcome of this might be a book, or even a series of books,

probably accompanied by taped materials, intended for language learners. Such a book may have a number of sections, each of which is likely to have a label referring to one, or more than one, discourse value. If we regard a 'course' as the implementation of a syllabus, we could not regard such a book as a 'coursebook'. This is not to say that the materials included could not be novel and interesting: there is no reason at all why they should not be. Nor am I suggesting that such books could not be a valuable aid to language learning. However, if I were to consider using such a book, I should want to understand clearly what the author's objectives were and, in order to understand this, I should need to know on what basis he had made certain decisions. Given that the number of speech acts may be indefinitely large, I should want to know what principles had guided the selection of some discourse value labels rather than others. Furthermore, I should want to know how and why he had made decisions about which linguistic units to include and which to omit: how he had made decisions about which linguistic units would, in the contexts provided, be associated with the selected discourse values.

The language syllabus: a relational approach

It would appear that the language syllabuses which exist at present have one important thing in common. They have, at their core, an item and unit inventory. The units included in that inventory may be grouped and labelled largely in terms of structural properties, or they may be grouped and labelled largely in terms of semantic properties. They may, or may not, be strictly ordered and graded according to certain linguistic and pedagogic criteria. However, if we wish to design a syllabus in such a way as to encourage the development of courses which concentrate not only on linguistic units in isolation, but on *related* linguistic units in context, then we must find a way of constructing syllabuses which are not constituted exclusively of item and unit inventories. I have suggested that we might initially approach this problem through a consideration of binary values. It has been noted that binary values are established through *relationships* between units in a discourse and that where these relationships are signalled lexico-syntactically, that signalling is simultaneously a signalling of unit values. It has also been noted that the words and expressions which signal such relationships may have an additional function: they may not only signal unit values, they may, by virtue of their grammatical properties, also signal unit weighting (or informational/stylistic focus). I have suggested that we might conceive of a syllabus in part as a series of *relational frames* — that is, as a series of frameworks, each of which is made up of a grouping of one — or, normally, more than one — pair of related values.

At this stage, because I have not yet discussed binary values in detail, it is not possible to provide anything approaching a comprehensive realization of the concept of relational frame. What it is possible to do, however, is to give some rough idea of what a relational frame would look like. Let us for the moment concentrate on the types of relational frame which might be constructed on the basis of a combination of two sets of binary relational values: General Causative (involving a *cause* member and an *effect* member) and Condition — Consequence. There are a number of ways in which the linguistic elements which might realize such relational values might be organized: each of these provides us with a possible relational frame. Three of these are outlined below:

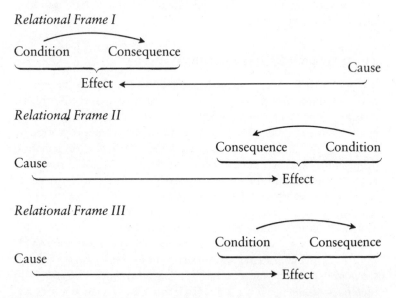

Frames like these, cannot, of course, constitute a syllabus. As they stand, they tell us almost nothing about the linguistic units which could be involved: all that they do tell us is that, whatever these units might be, they will bear a certain specific type of relationship to one another and that their sequential ordering will be related to their value assignment. In the construction of these frames, however, we have imposed certain linguistic restrictions. There are certain ways of linguistically realizing a General Causative relationship which are, in fact, not grammatically possible where General Causative and Condition — Consequence co-occur. We could at this point impose further restrictions by indexing the Condition — Consequence relationship with a label specifying that it is a specific *type* of Condition — Consequence relationship. We could, for example, specify that the condition must be a *realizable open condition*. The inclusion of this specification would mean, in broad terms, that the relationship cannot be realized by the grammatical forms associated with what are often referred to in language teaching circles as the *second conditional* and the *third conditional*. That is, the realization of the first member of the Condition — Consequence relation must not have a Past Simple or Past Perfect verbal group (e.g. *'If he arrived'/'If he had arrived'). The realization of the second member of the relation must not have a verbal group made up of a past tense modal plus the *base* form of the lexical verb or a Present Perfect construction (e.g. *'I would/ should leave/have left'). Indexation of this type is a convenient shorthand way of imposing certain realization restrictions. Similarly, we could index the General Causative relation in such a way as to specify that it should include only the Reason — Result realization of the Grounds — Conclusion relation. This means simply that the *cause* will be expressed as a reason and the *effect* as a result, and that the Grounds — Conclusion and Means — Result realizations of the General Causative relation (see Chapter 2), will be excluded.

Indexed frames such as I have suggested still do not constitute a syllabus. If the course writer is to make use of them, he must have some additional information. What form could such additional information take? I would suggest that it could take the form of *relational cues*, that is, of a list of words and expressions which may signal the relationships cited. However, there are a great many different ways (see Crombie 1985) in which most relationships of this sort may be signalled. Therefore, we must at this stage make a choice of which to include. On the basis of what criteria can we make such a choice? There are a number of different criteria that we might use (see Chapter 5). However, there is no reason in principle why we should not use, at least in part, the same sort of criteria which have traditionally been associated with structural syllabuses. These criteria might involve, for example, the notions of contrastive difficulty or stylistic appropriateness.

Let us assume that we have now applied whatever criteria we deem appropriate in the selection of relational cues. We could at this point put the relational frames and the relational cues together. We have now imposed quite a number of restrictions on the course writer and, in doing so, have given him some sort of guidance. On the basis of this guidance, he will be in a position to begin to think about the type of linguistic units which he might include at this point in his course. We have now provided the elements of part of a syllabus which might look something like this:

Relational Frame I

*Realizable Open Condition

Relational cues

If . . . , (then) . . . because . . .
If . . . , (then) . . . The reason (is)/(being) . . .
If . . . , (then) . . . The reason for X (is)/(being) . . .
If . . . , (then) X will mean that . . . because . . .
If . . . , (then) X will result in Y because . . .
If . . . , (then) X will result in (my) doing Y because . . .
In the event of (+ nominalization), (then) . . . because . . .

Relational Frame II

*Realizable Open Condition

Relational cues

Because . . . , . . . if . . .
. . . so . . . if . . .
. . . so . . . in the event of X
. . . so . . . in the event of (his) doing/not doing X
. . . so . . . providing that X
. . . so . . . providing that (he) does/doesn't do X

Relational Frame III

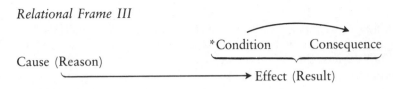

Cause (Reason)

*Realizable Open Condition

Relational cues

Because . . . , if . . . (then) . . .
Because . . . , if . . . (then) X will result in Y
Because . . . , if . . . (then) X will result in (my) doing Y
Because . . . , unless . . . (then) . . .

At this point, I should point out that exactly the combination of frames and cues illustrated above is not likely to occur as part of any particular syllabus. It is intended merely to illustrate in broad terms what sort of thing is meant by the term *relational syllabus.* However, if such a combination of frames and cues were actually to occur as part of a syllabus, it would provide course writers with a fairly substantial amount of guidance. There are a large number of implicit and explicit lexical, syntactic and semantic specifications. It is quite possible, however, to be a great deal more specific. One could, for example, include further modality and tense/aspect specifications at specific points within the relational cues. One could indicate where certain types of negation might occur or whether *will* or *going to* (or *intend to* or *plan to*, etc.) might occur in the realization of the Consequence member of the Condition — Consequence relation. One could, additionally, include a list of the various types of lexical items which might occur (e.g. items of clothing), or a list of specific lexical items.

At this stage, I should make it clear that I am not proposing that a unit inventory should not be part of a language syllabus: merely that it is doubtful whether a unit inventory should, of itself, constitute a syllabus. There could be a great deal of value in concentrating the attention of learners from time to time on units in isolation. Indeed, there is no reason at all why we should not make direct provision for this within what is otherwise a relational syllabus. Furthermore, although I have emphasized here that, by their nature, *unitary* discourse values are extremely difficult — if not impossible — to account for in a systematic way, it seems to be the case that certain unitary discourse values tend to be associated with certain binary discourse values or certain co-occurrences of binary discourse values. For example, the *reason* member of a Reason — Result binary pair often occurs as part of a sequence which has the unitary value *suggestion* (e.g. You should go because...). This means that it may be useful to index our relational frames from time to time with certain unitary discourse value labels, thus indicating to course writers that particular co-occurrences of binary values suggest an environment in which certain linguistic units might readily be associated with particular unitary discourse values. This sort of indexation would simply ensure that unitary discourse value is not lost sight of in the syllabus. It would not be a way of accounting for unitary discourse values in a systematic way.

2   General semantic relations

It is now commonly accepted among linguists that people communicating in language do not do so simply by means of individual words or sentences but by means of texts.

Werlich, *A text grammar of English*

No unit of experience can be understood out of context. Part of what a unit *is* is its relationship to other units.

Young, Becker, and Pike, *Rhetoric: discovery and change*

The importance of context

Underlying the theory of semantic relations is the observation that when we communicate with one another through language, we do not do so simply by means of individual words or clauses or even of individual sentences. We communicate by means of coherent stretches of interrelated clauses and sentences, the meaning of each of which can be *fully* understood only in relation to the context (both linguistic and non-linguistic) in which it occurs.

Since the full meaning of an utterance can be determined only in relation to its context, snatches of overheard conversation — in a restaurant or on a bus, for example — often have incomplete meanings. Because, as far as the unintended hearer is concerned, they are out of context, they are full of unfulfilled expectations. For this reason, the unintended hearer may find them more engaging than the participants themselves do. If you overheard someone say: 'So I just went up to my landlady and told her what I thought of her', the obvious question to ask, if social conventions allowed, would be: 'Why?' (The information that you do not have is the *reason* for the speaker's action.) At this stage in this particular conversation it is very unlikely that the reason will be revealed: the 'so' with which the overheard fragment began indicates that the reason has already been supplied. What is likely, however, is that if the participants in the discourse are sufficiently engaged or interested, one of them will ask your next question for you: 'What did she do then?' ('What was the *result* of your action?') Even if this question is not asked, you know from experience that, unless someone else takes the floor or the speaker gets side-tracked, he or she is likely to supply the information that that question would have elicited. If this information eludes you, then your expectations will remain unfulfilled.

The creation and fulfilment of expectations is a crucial part of spoken and written communication. This being the case, it is likely that the interest-creating tension of snatches of overheard conversation is due, at least in part, to the fact that the listener-in never knows whether or not his expectations will be satisfied. Researchers in the area of semantic relations are concerned not only with the creation of these expectations in themselves but also with the contribution that they make towards the interpretation of meaning.

Too little attention was paid in the past (by both linguists and society at large) to the apparently rather commonplace observation that the meaning of an utterance is affected by its context. It is because this fact is so often either ignored altogether or actually exploited that there are so many court cases involving decontextualization. Celebrities often take legal action against newspapers which they claim have misled their readers by quoting part rather than all of what was said or written on a particular occasion. We are all familiar, too, with occasions when politicians have quoted part of a speech made by a political opponent, removing it from the context which is crucial for accurate interpretation. Because the quotation is out of context, the impression which it conveys may be entirely different from the one intended by the original speaker. We are so used to this happening, that many of us make allowance for it, accepting it as a normal part of political life. If, however, courts of law were involved, their attitude would be less indulgent. It may be partly for this reason that politicians in Britain, speaking within the House of Commons, are, under most circumstances, protected from court action being taken against them.

In courts of law, general situational context (including non-verbal gestures such as nods, winks, nudges etc.), as well as specific linguistic context (co-text), are treated not as a possible source of circumstantial mitigation, but as prime evidence. In cases of defamation and misrepresentation, context is of prime importance to both prosecution and defence. The reason for this is not hard to find. In the absence of co-text, the statement 'You can't trust a word that he says', appears to be an unambiguous assertion of someone's dishonesty. With linguistic context supplied, however, it may be interpreted as a statement of an entirely different kind: 'You can't trust a word that he says because his comments are so often ironic.'

Making sense of linguistic expressions in context

If someone said to you (or you overheard someone say): 'That bully hit the child. She fell down', you would almost certainly assume that the two statements were not juxtaposed by accident — that the speaker, in putting the two statements together, intended to convey something about their meaning. In this case, you would infer that the referent of 'she' was 'the child' and that the two statements are in a cause-effect relation; that the *effect* of the bully's hitting the child was that the child fell down. If what the speaker said was: 'That bully hit the child so she fell down', you would know for sure that, in the speaker's opinion, there was a definite cause-effect connection between the two events. There are lots of signals like *so* (for example, *however, yet, consequently, similarly*), that tell us that certain kinds of meaning relations underlie clauses and sentences. A sentence like: 'He consequently felt terrible' would seem completely unnatural if it were not placed after a sentence giving the *reason* for the feeling, such as: 'He failed his final exams.'

In the first example that I gave ('That bully hit the child. She fell down'), the relation between the statements was implicit. Your knowledge of the relation between things, events and abstractions in the world leads you to assume that it exists even in the absence of an explicit signal such as *'because'*. This assumption is an important part of your interpretation of the meaning of the two statements. Although, however, in this case the relation between the statements was not made explicit, we can see that it could have been. The speaker might have said, for example:

Because that bully hit the child, she fell down.
or
That bully hit the child *so* she fell down.
or
The child fell down. The *reason* was that that bully hit her.

Certain ways of linking clauses and sentences are more explicit in terms of defining the relationship between them than others: *because* and *although*, for example, are more explicit than *but*. *Because* is an explicit signal of a specific type of cause-effect relationship (i.e. the General Causative — see page 39), *although* is an explicit signal of the Concession — Contraexpectation relation (see page 37). In example 1, the information in the second clause is presented as being unexpected in the light of the information in the first:

1 Although he's a crook, I trust him.
(Concession — Contraexpectation)

And and *but* indicate relationship in a more general sense. As can be seen in examples 2–7, the co-ordinator *and* may link clauses which bear several quite different types of relationship to one another:

2 He's got brown hair and he's wearing a blazer.
(Coupling — see page 40)
3 She ran to the bus stop and got on the Number 41.
(Chronological Sequence — see page 40)
4 He missed the bus and arrived late for work.
(General Causative: Reason — Result — see page 39)
5 A: Are they good at the same sort of things?
  B: Yes. He's good at tennis and she plays squash well.
(Simple Comparison — see page 38)
6 A: In what sense are their views different?
  B: He believes in democracy and she's committed to autocracy.
(Simple Contrast — see page 37)
7 There's no point in explaining it to him. He has sailed from England to Australia and he's convinced that the earth is flat.
(Concession — Contraexpectation — see page 37)

The co-ordinator *but* is somewhat more relationally specific than is *and*. *But* generally signals that there is some contrastive relationship between the two conjuncts. It does not, however, signal a specific type of contrastive relationship:

8 John's work is marvellous but Tim's is terrible.
9 He's a crook but I trust him.

In 8 and 9, the presence of *but* suggests that some sort of contrastive relationship is involved. If we are to be more specific about the particular type of contrastive relationship involved in each case, then we must look for other clues. Because we are likely to regard crooks as untrustworthy, most of us will treat the content of the second clause in 9 as being unexpected in the light of the content of the first and will, therefore, interpret the relationship between them as being that of Concession — Contraexpectation (c.f. example 1 above). Since there is no obvious counterexpectation in 8, we are likely to interpret the relationship between the clauses as being that of Simple Contrast where two things (i.e. the work of two people) are compared in respect of the difference in quality ('marvellous' *versus* 'terrible') between them. However, the co-text or the situational context in which 8 occurs might supply the evidence that will lead to a different relational interpretation. For example, if we know that 'John' and 'Tim' are identical twins, that they are regarded as being intelligent, that they both attend the same school (which is considered to be a good one), that they are taught by the same teacher (who is highly competent), and that there is no apparent reason why the work of one should be substantially different in quality from the work of the other, then we are likely to interpret the relationship between the two clauses in 8 as being that of Concession — Contraexpectation.

We have already seen that some words and phrases are more explicit in terms of signalling relationship than others. We saw that *although* and *because* signal specific types of relationship, that *but* generally signals contrast (but not a specific *type* of contrastive relationship), and that *and* may co-ordinate clauses between which there are relationships of a number of quite different types. This raises a very important issue. Where relationships are not clearly signalled, how do we determine that a speaker or writer intends that we should infer a relationship at all, let alone a specific type of relationship? Although this question raises very complex and detailed problems for the linguist, it is possible to provide at least part of the answer in a general and fairly straightforward way. Indeed, some of the examples that we have looked at so far clearly demonstrate the importance of a number of factors including juxtaposition, sequencing, lexical selection and general assumptions about or knowledge of, the world in general, the participants in the discourse themselves, or the type of social activity in which the discourse participants are involved.

Let us begin by considering the importance of juxtaposition. As I mentioned earlier in this chapter, where two sentences are juxtaposed, we make the assumption that this juxtaposition is in some sense informative: that the speaker or writer, in juxtaposing them, intends to convey something meaningful about them. However, although juxtaposition leads us to infer relationship, it does not, in itself, tell us anything about the *type* of relationship involved. The relationships between the sentences in 10–14 are clearly different:

10 That bully hit the child. She fell down.
11 John's work is marvellous. Tim's is terrible.
12 John's work is marvellous. Tim's is great too.
13 John arrived late for work. He missed the train.
14 John ran to the bus stop. He got on the Number 41.

If we look at the examples above in the light of the sequencing of units, we begin to appreciate more clearly the factors involved in relational interpretation. Where events are involved, then sequencing may be important. Thus, our cultural knowledge leads us to suppose that the events outlined in the two sentences in example 14 above are in sequence and, therefore, to infer a relationship of Chronological Sequence (i.e. one event following the other in time) between them. Unless there is some linguistic indication that the sequential ordering of linguistic units does not reflect the sequential ordering of events, we would not expect to find a linguistic sequence such as that in the example below:

15 *John got on the Number 41. He ran to the bus stop.

Events are also involved in examples 10 and 13 above. Here, however, our knowledge of the world leads us to suppose that there is more than a temporal relationship involved. We all know that people — particularly small people — may fall down as a result of being hit and, if we live in a particular type of environment, we know that people may be late for work as a result of missing a train. We therefore assume, in the absence of any information to the contrary, that there is a causal relationship between the events outlined. Where a temporal and a causal relation co-exist, it is quite acceptable, in English at least, to reverse the sequencing of the propositions:

16 The child fell down. That bully hit her.

In each of examples 10, 13 and 14, there is a further clue to the fact that there is some relationship between the events outlined in the juxtaposed sentences. This clue is a referential one. In each case, an item in the second sentence makes anaphoric reference to an item in the first. A word or expression is said to be *anaphoric* where it picks out the same entity (or entities) as is picked out by some prior word or expression in the discourse. Thus, the pronoun 'she' in example 10 is anaphoric: it refers to 'the child'. Likewise, the pronoun 'he' in examples 13 and 14 is anaphoric.

Anaphora is not the only type of reference. Another is deixis. The word *deixis* is used to describe the linguistic encoding of various aspects of situational context. Thus, if the demonstrative 'that' ('that bully') in example 10 refers to someone within visual range who is being indicated by the speaker, then it will be described as deictic. There are several types of deixis: *person deixis*, *place deixis*, *time deixis*, *discourse deixis* and *social deixis*. I shall refer briefly to the first four of these here. An interesting and far more detailed discussion of deixis is provided by Levinson (1983: Chapter 1).

We use the term 'person deixis' to refer to the linguistic encoding of the roles of the participants in a particular speech event. In English (see example 17), person deixis is encoded by pronouns and their predicate agreements:

17 *I*'m fat but *you*'re thin.

The term *place deixis* refers to the encoding of spatial locations relative to the location of discourse participants. Place deixis is commonly encoded in demonstratives and deictic adverbs of place (see example 18):

18 I'll put *this* one *here* and *that* one *there*.

The encoding of temporal points and spans relative to the time at which an utterance takes place is referred to as *time deixis*. Time deixis may be encoded in deictic adverbs of time (e.g. *now*, *then*, *last week*) and in tense (see example 19):

19 I *left yesterday* and John *leaves tomorrow*.

Finally, *discourse deictics* refer to the portions of an unfolding discourse. Thus, for example, *in the last paragraph* is discourse deictic. I have already mentioned that many words and phrases (e.g. *therefore*, *however*, *because*) may signal relationships between textual elements and, therefore, identify discourse values. These words and phrases are discourse deictic: they indicate relationship between one unit of discourse and another. (Discourse deictics have been discussed by a large number of linguists and philosophers including Grice 1975; Fillmore 1975; Wilson 1975; Lyons 1977; Levinson 1979b; Winter 1977. Of these, only Winter's discussion is directly related to semantic relational realization.)

Both anaphora and discourse deixis are cohesive devices: they are devices which link various parts of a text. Cohesive devices can play an important role in the realization of semantic relationships. The role which they play, as in the case, for example, of the anaphoric pronouns and the co-ordinator *and*, may be a general one: they may indicate the presence of a relationship without actually specifying the type of relationship involved. They may, on the other hand, as in the case of some subordinators such as *because*, indicate the actual nature of the relationship involved. Cohesive devices are, as we have seen, of various different types. Cohesion (about which there is a detailed discussion in Halliday and Hasan 1976) may, for example, involve conjuctions, pronouns and anaphoric lexical items (e.g. *the man* ← *the idiot*). It may also involve substitution (see example 20), or ellipsis (see example 21):

20 He runs more quickly than she does.

21 He's intelligent but she isn't ____.

Cohesion, then, plays an important role in the recognition and identification of semantic relationships. The actual choice of lexical items (both within the related units of discourse themselves, and in their co-text) may also be important. If you look again at example 11, you will see that the selection of the lexical items 'marvellous' and 'terrible', within the framework of sentences which are cohesively linked, is relationally significant. The words 'marvellous' and 'terrible' are clearly contrastive here. However, it would have been equally possible to indicate contrast by negating one of these lexical items within a cohesive linguistic environment (see example 22):

22 John's work is marvellous. Tim's isn't.

Looking again at example 11, we can see that if we were to replace 'terrible' by 'great' (c.f. example 12), we could not be sure, in the absence of a contrastive (e.g. *but*) or comparative (e.g. *also*) signal, whether 'John' and 'Tim' are being compared in respect of similarity (Simple Comparison), or difference (Simple Contrast).

We have seen, in discussing example 11, that lexical selection *within* the related units of discourse may be relationally significant. Lexical selection within the *co-text* of related linguistic units may also be relationally significant. Thus, in examples 5 and 6, the occurrence of 'same' and 'different' in the co-text is clearly an important aspect of relational interpretation.

In looking at examples 10, 13 and 14, we saw that knowledge of a particular type of cultural environment or general knowledge of the relationships between events in the world may play a role in the identification of a specific type of relationship. Our awareness of the actual social activity which provides the situational context for a particular discourse may also be relevant. Thus, for example, if A in example 23 is uttered by a school teacher in the context of a classroom lesson, the pupil to whom it is addressed will probably interpret it as a command to stop talking rather than as an Elicitation requiring a Reply providing a reason:

23 A: Why are you laughing?

An awareness of the type of social activity taking place may not, however, be sufficient. There are occasions when interpretation requires specific knowledge about the actual participants in the discourse. Thus, a knowledge of the fact that the speaker has a friend called Anna Lloyd who produces abstract expressionist paintings would help in the relational interpretation of 24:

24 I like abstract expressionism. I hate Anna Lloyd's.

Most of what I have said so far applies to discourses of any type. When we look in particular at conversational discourse, then it may be helpful to make reference to some of the arguments which Grice (1975/1978) has put forward. Grice has argued that, in interpreting conversation, we must make certain assumptions concerning the co-operativeness of the participants. He has suggested that there are four basic principles (or *maxims of conversation*) which underlie the efficient co-operative use of language. These four maxims, taken together, express a *general co-operative principle* which can be summarized as follows:

> Speakers should speak sincerely (Maxim of Quality), relevantly (Maxim of Relevance) and clearly — that is, in an orderly and unambiguous way — (Maxim of Manner), and should provide adequate, but not unnecessary, information (Maxim of Quantity).

Grice argues that, wherever possible, hearers will interpret what we say as conforming to these maxims on at least some level. The interpretative inferences that they make arise from their attempts to apply the principles of co-operative interaction. Thus, for example, an utterance by a different speaker which follows a *why* question, will generally be interpreted as providing a *reason*. In the first exchange below (example 25), the presence of *because* ensures that speaker A will have no difficulty in interpreting B's contribution as a reply giving a reason. In the second exchange, however, (example 26), there is no explicit relational signal present:

25 A: Why did he do it?
    B: Because he didn't have any money.

26 A: Why did John do it?
  B: People hate being bullied.

It is likely that, in interpreting B's contribution in example 26, speaker A will, initially at least, make the assumption that speaker B is not deviating from the co-operative principle and, therefore, that his contribution is relevant and informative. This being the case, he will be inclined to interpret B's contribution (as in example 25) as a reply giving a reason. He will, therefore, call upon whatever relevant background information is available to him which might suggest that whatever John did could have been done in response to bullying. The interpretative inference made by speaker A in this case is based on his assumption that speaker B is actually *observing* the maxims of conversation. There are, of course, many occasions on which speakers will deliberately *flout* these maxims in order to achieve a particular effect. Thus, the irony of B's response in example 27 below, comes about through the deliberate flouting of the co-operative principle:

27 A: Why did you take my pen?
  B: I had one of my own already.

The co-operative principle as expressed in Grice's four maxims has been extended by two further maxims — the *maxim of informativeness* (Atlas and Levinson 1981), and the *maxim of politeness* (Brown and Levinson 1978). Furthermore, researchers involved in crosscultural studies of language usage (e.g. Bauman and Sherzer 1974) argue that there seem to be inference rules which operate to assign functions to utterances partly on the basis of social roles and expectations (see the discussion of example 23).

Although there is little doubt that assumptions concerning the co-operativeness of participants in a conversation and assumptions concerning social roles and expectations do play an important part in the ability of hearers to make certain types of inference (see Levinson 1983: Chapters 3 and 6), it seems to me that, as far as semantic relational inferences are concerned, intonation may be even more important. This is discussed in Crombie 1985.

Semantic relations between propositions versus 'role' relations

Terms such as Reason — Result and Concession — Contraexpectation are descriptive labels which identify underlying semantic relationships which provide the underpinning of all coherent stretches of language extending beyond the expression of a single proposition. Semantic relationships of this type are relationships between two elements of a discourse, each of which has, by virtue of the particular type of relationship involved, a particular discourse value. Each of the discourse elements involved in such a relationship is referred to as one of the *members* of the relation. Thus, as I pointed out in Chapter 1, the identification of a particular semantic relation (e.g. General Causative: Reason — Result) is simultaneously an identification of a related pair of discourse values (e.g. *reason* and *result*). Semantic relationships of the type I have been discussing involve, minimally, two propositions. Thus, for example, the two propositions 'John is intelligent'/ 'Tim is perceptive', may be related in a number of different ways, as in examples 28 and 29:

28 A: What's the difference between them?
    B: John is intelligent; Tim is perceptive.
29 A: How are they similar?
    B: John is intelligent; Tim is perceptive.

There *are* relationships which exist within a single proposition. These are referred to as *role* (or *case*) relations. Role relations are relationships between the predicate of a single proposition (normally encoded as a verb or verbal group) and its argument or arguments (usually encoded as a noun or nominal group). The predicate of the proposition *John ran* is *ran*, and its argument is *John*. The argument *John* bears an agentive relationship to the predicate *ran*: that is, it may be described as performing the role of *agent* (the doer of the action) within the proposition. Role relations are relationships *within* a single proposition. They are essentially different in kind from the semantic relations *between* propositions with which I am concerned here. I have, however discussed them elsewhere (Crombie 1985).

Semantic relational membership

The semantic relations with which I am here concerned involve, minimally, two propositions and, therefore, because the clause is very often the linguistic unit which encodes a single proposition, each member of a semantic relation is often encoded as a separate clause. However, a semantic relational member need not be encoded as a single clause: it may be encoded as a group of clauses and, in certain circumstances, it may be encoded as a unit embedded within a clause.

The semantic relational member as a group of clauses

Within a discourse, there may be a whole complex of interacting semantic relationships. For example, two clauses, each of which constitutes one member of a semantically related pair, may, taken together, constitute one member of a further semantic relational pair:

30 John's clever and Mary is clever too but Simon is brilliant.

$$\text{Simple Comparison}$$

$$\text{Simple Contrast}$$

Furthermore, a single clause may constitute one member of two different semantic relational pairings:

31 John's going but Sue isn't because her son is ill.

$$\text{Simple Contrast}$$

$$\text{Result —— Reason}$$

We have seen that one member of a semantically related pair may be made up of more than one clause. In fact, many clauses, taken together, may constitute one member of a particular semantic relationship:

32 *John's playing squash and Mary's weeding the garden whilst Tim's chopping wood and Sam's preparing the dinner* but *Jane isn't doing anything.*

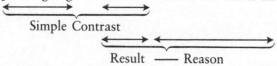

The co-ordinator *but* in 32 suggests that there is contrast. In order to identity the actual semantic relation involved, it would be necessary to make reference to context.

The semantic relational member as a unit embedded within a clause

There are occasions when both members of a semantic relationship between propositions may be present within a single clause. This can happen only where more than one proposition is encoded by a single clause. Such encoding requires some form of *propositional embedding.* Two propositions are encoded by a single clause in example 33, where the nominalization 'his exaggeration' encodes the proposition 'he exaggerates':

33 His exaggeration makes her furious.
(i.e. 'he exaggerates' (Reason) ⎫
      'she becomes furious' (Result) ⎬ Reason — Result
                                    ⎭

A note on semantic relational realization and language learning

My concern so far has been with the fact that there are underlying semantic relationships (e.g. Simple Contrast) between discourse elements. These relationships provide the semantic underpinning for — and are, therefore, a *necessary* aspect of — the interpretation of all coherent stretches of language which extend beyond the expression of a single proposition. And, since it is not often that a communication ends with the expression of a single proposition, our understanding of these relationships is clearly an important aspect of our understanding of the dynamics of linguistic communication. Further, there appears to be a finite, and, indeed, a quite manageable (as far as language teaching is concerned) number of different types of semantic relation, and these different types appear to have cross-linguistic validity. That is, they appear to be realizable — although often in quite different ways — in all languages. Not only, however, may semantic relations be realized through the lexical and grammatical systems of *different languages* in different ways, each type of semantic relation may be realized in *the same language* in different ways. Both of these facts are clearly relevant as far as language learning is concerned.

Whether or not a particular semantic relation is, on a particular occasion, implicit or linguistically explicit carries certain communicative implications. Where a semantic relation is made linguistically explicit, the particular way in which this explicitness is achieved will have important stylistic and informational implications. When we look at a particular type of discourse (for example, varieties of scientific report), we can see that an important aspect of the communicative dynamics of that discourse is the variety and distribution of relational types together with the various different ways in which each relational type is realized.

As can be seen in the examples below, when propositions are encoded in clauses and sentences and embedded constructions, the information in them can be focused in different ways. Thus, for example, one of the members of a relation involving Concession — Contraexpectation can be co-ordinated to the other (see example 34), or subordinated to it (see example 35), or the two members may occur in separate juxtaposed sentences[1] (see example 36):

34 He's a crook but she trusts him.
35 Although he's a crook, she trusts him.
36 He's a crook. She trusts him, nevertheless.

The same thing applies in the case of the members of a relation of Chronological Sequence. Example 40 illustrates the fact that certain types of linguistic realization may allow for a reversal of the usual sequential ordering of propositions:

37 He sat down and (then) he picked up the newspaper.
38 Having sat down, he picked up the newspaper.
39 He sat down. Afterwards, he picked up the newspaper.
40 He picked up the newspaper after having sat down.

The most important point that arises out of the observation that the same semantic relation may be realized in the same language in a number of different ways is that it provides the syllabus designer with the possibility of introducing grammatical constructions in a way that is both systematic and discourse motivated. A brief consideration of Reason —. Result should be sufficient to demonstrate that this is the case. First, let us consider some of the items that may signal Reason — Result. These include *subordinators* such as *because, as, since, seeing (that)*; *prepositions* such as *because of, due to, in view of, thanks to*; *causative verbs* such as *cause, bring about, effect*, and *nouns* such as *result, reason, consequence*. Each type of signal may occur in a range of structural environments a few of which are illustrated in the following list of examples:

41 Calypso released Odysseus because Hermes ordered it.
42 Because Hermes ordered that Odysseus be released, Calypso released him.
43 Because Hermes ordered the release of Odysseus, Calypso released him.
44 Hermes ordered the release of Odysseus and, because he did so, Calypso released him.
45 It was because Hermes ordered it that Calypso released Odysseus.
46 Hermes ordered the release of Odysseus and so Calypso released him.

47 Because of Hermes' order, Calypso released Odysseus.
48 Because of an order given by Hermes, Calypso released Odysseus.
49 Hermes' order caused Calypso to release Odysseus.
50 Hermes' order resulted in the release of Odysseus by Calypso.
51 Calypso released Odysseus. The reason was that Hermes ordered it.
52 Calypso released Odysseus, the reason being that Hermes ordered it.
53 The reason why Calypso released Odysseus was that Hermes had ordered it.

We can see, then, that each type of signal may be associated with a range of structures and, therefore, that the selection of a particular signal within the environment of a particular relational frame has implications as far as the introduction or consolidation of structures is concerned. Of course, the examples above give only a very limited indication of the grammatical range which is made available to us within the framework of Reason — Result. A whole range of additional constructions may be involved, some of which are illustrated in the examples below:

54 He was praised for his forbearance.
55 He was struck for begging in the hall.
56 He was so careful that he didn't reveal his identity.
57 He was too afraid to remain there.
58 He was not strong enough to draw the bow.
59 Being the king, Alcinous received Odysseus.
60 Relieved at their reaction to his skills, Odysseus rejoiced.

The last four examples, 61–64, illustrate some of the ways in English in which a subsidiary or additional reason may be encoded:

61 Put it down: it's too heavy for you anyway.
62 I won't touch it: it's foul in any case.
63 You might as well go. You'd be useless here anyway.
64 Don't go near it: it's dangerous. Besides, it's filthy.

Examples 61–64 not only demonstrate something of the constructional range which may be associated with a particular semantic relation, they also demonstrate the importance of cohesion (see pages 26–8 ff.) in semantic relational realization.

There are two important considerations which must be taken into account in designing a relational syllabus and which I have not so far referred to. First, it must be borne in mind that the same construction realizing the same semantic relations may, depending on its lexical content, involve different semantic roles. This is illustrated in examples 65 and 66:

65 Her intervention led to his defeat.
   (i.e. She intervened and he was defeated (by someone))
66 Her intervention led to his despair.
   (i.e. She intervened and he experienced despair)

Secondly, it is important that, in considering spoken discourse, the syllabus designer should take into account the role played by intonation and, in particular, the role played by intonation in semantic relational recognition (see Crombie 1985).

If, then, semantic relations are language universals — that is, if all human languages have the same underlying semantic relations which are based on our perceptions of the relationships between things, events and abstractions in time and space — then it follows that these relations will be conceptually familiar to language students and should provide an appropriate semantic framework for the presentation of new grammatical constructions or the revision of already familiar ones in which the members of particular semantic relations may be variously realized. The presentation and revision of grammatical constructions within semantic relational frameworks is likely to have two main advantages. First, it is likely to encourage learners to concentrate on the communicative function of grammar by bringing together, at a particular point in the syllabus, certain different constructions through which a single, underlying semantic relation may be realized. Particularly where learners have been following a purely structural syllabus, these different constructions may have previously seemed to them to be entirely unrelated functionally. Secondly, the presentation of grammatical constructions within relational frames is likely to encourage learners to develop an awareness of the stylistic and informational implications of grammatical choice. These points can be more readily appreciated when considered in the context of the outline of general semantic relations that follows.

An outline of general semantic relations

COMPARISON/CONTRAST

All of the relations collected under this general heading are concerned with making comparisons or contrasts between things or between utterances. That is, they are concerned with looking at ways in which things or utterances are similar to, or different from, one another.

There are a number of different relations involving contrast. First, there is *Simple Contrast*, where the difference between two things is simply pointed out. So, in the following example, men and women are contrasted in terms of the effect that lust allegedly has on them:

> *They say that lust makes a man old* but *keeps a woman young.* They say a lot of nonsense.
>
> Chandler, *The Long Good-Bye*

Simple Contrast is the most common type of contrast, but there are others. Two of these (Statement — Denial and Denial — Correction) involve denying or correcting what someone else has said or may have assumed. In the extract below, there is a relation of *Statement — Denial* (i.e. 'And I need not detain you any longer' — 'You're not detaining me'), and a relation of *Denial — Correction* (i.e. 'You're not detaining me. — I'm detaining you'):

> 'I think you are a very stupid person. You look stupid. You are in a stupid business. You have a stupid mission.'
> 'I get it,' I said. 'I'm stupid. It sank in after a while.'
> '*And I need not detain you any longer.*'
> '*You're not detaining me. I'm detaining you.*'
>
> Chandler, *Farewell, My Lovely*

The next relation involving contrast is often signalled in English by *though* or *although*. In this relation, which may be referred to as *Concession — Contraexpectation* (or Expectancy Reversal), an inference which might be drawn on the basis of the content of the first member of the relation, is blocked in the second member:

> Common sense is the little man in a grey suit who never makes a mistake in addition. But it's always somebody else's money he's adding up.
>
> Chandler, *Playback*

There are two other fairly common types of contrastive relation. In the first of these, *Contrastive Alternation* (see the example below), a choice is offered between two opposite possibilities:

I sat down and rolled a cigarette around in my fingers and waited. *She either knew something* or *she didn't*. If she knew something, *she either would tell me* or *she wouldn't*. It was that simple.

Chandler, *Farewell, My Lovely*

The last type of contrast that I shall introduce here, that is, *Statement — Exception*, is illustrated in the extract below:

Cops are like a doctor that gives you an aspirin for a brain tumor, except that the cop would rather cure it with a blackjack.

Chandler, *The Long Good-Bye*

So far, I have introduced a number of semantic relations which are defined in contrastive terms. I shall now introduce a number of semantic relations which may be defined in terms of comparison or similarity. In the first of these, *Simple Comparison*, two things (or abstractions), are compared in respect of some similarity between them:

She adores music and when the New York Philharmonic is playing Hindemith she can tell you which one of the six bass viols came in a quarter of a beat too late. I hear Toscanini can also.

Chandler, *The Long Good-Bye*

In Simple Comparison, two things (or abstractions) are compared; in the other four relations which involve comparison, it is not things, but utterances, which may be compared in respect of the similarity between them. These four relations are labelled: Statement — Affirmation, Statement — Exemplification, Paraphrase, and Amplification. In *Statement — Affirmation*, one speaker affirms (e.g. 'Quite so', 'I agree') what has been said by another speaker. In *Statement — Exemplification*, a general statement in the first member of the relation is illustrated by an example in the second. In *Paraphrase*, the same content is expressed in two propositions in different ways. In *Amplification*, a general term in the first member of the relation is specified in the second (e.g. Someone invited me. That someone was you.).

There are three types of Amplification. In the first (Term Specification), a specific term is substituted for a general one (see first example below). In the second (Predicate Specification), one member of the relation amplifies the other by specifying the content of its verbal predicate (see second example below). In the third

(Term Exemplification), a general term is illustrated with reference to a particular (see third example below):

> Paris seized someone. It was Helen.

> He said/knew that Hector was dead.

> All long battles, the Trojan war for example, have several reversals of fortune.

CAUSE — EFFECT

Each of the three relations considered in this section is concerned in a general way with cause and effect. In the *Condition — Consequence* relation, the condition may be either realizable (i.e. open to realization), or unrealizable (i.e. not open to realization). In the first extract below, the conditions are realizable; in the second, the condition is unrealizable:

> I just know that she is a lonely and frightened and unhappy girl. When I know why, *if I do manage to find out, I'll let you know or I won't. If I don't you'll just have to throw the book at me.*

> Chandler, *Playback*

> Common sense is the Monday morning quarterback who *could have won the ball game if he had been on the team.*

> Chandler, *Playback*

In the *Means — Purpose* relation, the purpose member outlines the action that is/was/will be undertaken with the intention of achieving a particular result:

> *I had been shot full of dope to keep me quiet.*
> *Perhaps scopolamine too, to make me talk.*

> Chandler, *Farewell, My Lovely*

The last of the relations to be included in this section is the *General Causative*. In this relation, there is a cause (which is not hypothetical), and an effect (which is not necessarily intended). The General Causative relation has three different realization types according to whether the causative member is presented as a *reason for* a particular result (Reason — Result), as a *means* by which a particular result is/was/will be achieved (Means — Result), or as a *basis* for a particular conclusion being reached (Grounds — Conclusion). In the extract below, there is a Reason — Result realization of General Causative in which the result member of the relation is made up of both members of a Condition — Consequence relation:

The other part of me wanted to get out and stay out but *this was the part I never listened to. Because if I ever had I would have stayed in the town where I was born and worked in the hardware store and married the boss's daughter* ...

Chandler, *The Long Good-Bye*

TEMPORAL

There are two temporal relations. In the first, the *Simultaneity* relation, two events overlap either wholly, or partly, in time. In the second, *Chronological Sequence* (illustrated below), one event follows another in time:

I put the liquor bottle away and went over to the wash-bowl to rinse the glass out. When I had done that I washed my hands and bathed my face in cold water and looked at it.

Chandler, *The Lady in the Lake*

COUPLING

In its most basic form, the *Coupling* relation may be described as a non-elective (i.e. not involving choice), non-sequential relationship between conjoined propositions:

Miss Vermilyea will advance you some expense money and pay you a retainer of $250.

Chandler, *Playback*

Coupling may, however, involve the assertion or implication that the information in the first member of the relation is inadequate or insufficient on its own (i.e. without the information in the second member). Constructions in English such as *not only ... but also, not ... let alone,* and *(not) even,* carry this implication. We may refer to this type of Coupling as Rhetorical Coupling:

He's not only a trained boxer,   he's also a sadist.

Additionally, there is a particular type of Coupling which involves contrast. This may be referred to as Contrastive Coupling:

He *tried to remember the details* but *failed.*

SUPPLEMENTARY ALTERNATION

The relation of *Supplementary Alternation* involves two or more choices or possibilities which are in some way related; they are not opposites but simply different options:

You could walk through the average cell block at night and look in through the bars and *see a huddle of brown blanket*, or *a head of hair*, or *a pair of eyes looking at nothing*.

Chandler, *The Long Good-Bye*

Note

Some linguists make a distinction between propositions (and, by extension, between semantic relations) in terms of *semantic rank*. Thus, for example, Beekman and Callow (1974) distinguish between developmental propositions (which are said to be of equal semantic rank within a discourse) and supporting propositions (which are said to be of lower semantic rank in a discourse than those which they are said to support). By extension, they argue that semantic relations are either additive (involving developmental propositions) or associative (involving a developmental and a supporting proposition). Likewise, Fuller (1959) makes a distinction between relations involving *equality of class* and relations involving *equality of support*. I believe that the term *semantic rank* is a misleading one which has resulted from a confusion between relationships themselves and their actual realizations. Rank is a grammatical, not a semantic phenomenon: it is not a property of propositions or of semantic relations, it is a property of the grammatical realization of semantically related propositions. Beekman and Callow (1974: 284) refer to Concession — Contraexpectation as an associative relation (i.e. as a relation involving a developmental member and a supporting member). Concession — Contraexpectation is, however, like all other semantic relations, neither an associative relation nor an additive relation. It may, however, have associative realizations (involving subordination, see example 3), or developmental realizations (involving independence or co-ordination, see examples 1 and 2):

1 He's a thief but she trusts him.
2 He's a thief. She trusts him nevertheless.
3 Although he's a thief, she trusts him.

3   Interactive semantic relations

The discussion in Chapter 2 centred on those semantic relations which occur in all types of discourse and which involve general discoursal values (henceforth referred to as *general semantic relations*). In this chapter, however, I shall be primarily concerned with conversational discourse and, in the examination of coherence in conversational discourse, the focus of attention moves from *general semantic relations* to *interactive semantic relations* (that is, to those semantic relations which involve interactional values).

Conversational exchanges: slots, moves, and acts

A minimal conversational exchange may be defined as a sequence of two related turns taken by different speakers, each turn consisting of a single move.

Utterances which occur as part of a conversation may have a number of different possible interactive functions within the discourse. They may (meta-statements) give advance information about a discourse topic (e.g. 'I'm going to talk about African politics today'), they may (macro-performatives) introduce what is to follow by expressing its illocutionary force (e.g. 'I'll give you some advice'/'Here's a warning'), or they may (conclusion) provide a summary of what has gone before (e.g. 'So those were all the political points'). Utterances such as *okay, well, right, so,* may function as boundary indicators (frames): they may indicate that the speaker regards one topic as over and is about to introduce another or, where they have falling tone and low pitch and occupy the whole of a speaker's turn, that he/she is prepared either to close the conversation or to accept a new conversational initiative from another speaker. Two such contiguous utterances by different speakers function as a preclosing exchange in a conversation and are likely to be followed by a closing exchange (Schegloff and Sacks 1973).

In the broadest structural terms, exchanges within an interactive

discourse can be seen in terms of *initiation*, *response* and, option-
ally, *follow-up*[1]:

1 A: Where's the book? (Initiation)
   B: It's on the table. (Response)
   A: Thanks. (Follow-up)

Some utterances, such as that of B in 2, are simultaneously
responding and initiating:

2 A: Where's the book? (Initiation)
   B: Isn't it on the table? (Response/Initiation)
   A: Oh yes, so it is. (Response)

There are, then, three types of structural slot within conversational exchanges: initiating slots, response slots and follow-up
slots. Within these structural slots, we find three types of move:
eliciting moves (which request information or action), *informing/
acting moves* (which supply information or in which an action is
undertaken), and *acknowledging moves* (which either acknowledge
a request for information/action, or acknowledge that information
has been given or action undertaken). Each conversational exchange contains at least one informing/acting move and, where this
involves information rather than action, it can occur *either* in the
initiating slot (see example 3), *or* in the responding slot (see
example 4):

3 A: Your client has arrived. (Informing move in initiating slot)
   B: Okay. (Acknowledging move in responding slot)
4 A: Where's the cat? (Eliciting move in initiating slot)
   B: It's downstairs. (Informing move in responding slot)
   A: Thanks. (Acknowledging move in follow-up slot)

An informing move in the initiating slot in an exchange requires
an acknowledging move (which may be non-verbal — nodding,
pointing etc.); an informing move in the responding slot need not
always be followed by an acknowledging move.

The actual realization of a move in conversational discourse is
referred to as an *act*:

An eliciting move is realized by either of the following acts:
Elicitation, *Directive*.

An acknowledging move is realized by the act referred to as
Acknowledge.

An informing/acting move may be realized by any of the following acts: *Informative, Replying Informative, Respond, React, Comment.*

These acts are defined below:

Elicitation(EL) (e.g. 'Where's the salt'/'Are you unhappy') is an act whose primary function is to request a linguistic response in the form of an Informative, although the actual response may be a non-verbal substitute such as a nod.

Directive(DIR) (e.g. 'Sit down'/'Don't sit down') is an act whose primary function is to request/require a non-linguistic response (i.e. carrying out or refraining from carrying out an action). Directives give information about a speaker's wishes/requirements (e.g. 'I want you (not) to do X'). The typically non-linguistic response to a Directive may be accompanied by (e.g. 'okay') or replaced by (e.g. 'I won't') a linguistic response.

Acknowledge(ACK) is a linguistic (e.g. 'yes', 'okay', 'fine', 'mm'), or a non-linguistic (e.g. a nod) response indicating that a preceding utterance or action has been noted. An Acknowledge may follow an Informative, a Replying Informative or a Directive, or it may occur as an accompaniment to a React.

Informative(INF) (e.g. 'There's an oak tree over there') is an act whose primary function is to pass on ideas, facts, opinions etc. Where an Informative relates directly to a preceding Elicitation, I shall refer to it as a *Replying Informative*(REP INF). A Replying Informative is the linguistic response appropriate to an Elicitation:

5 A: Where's your hat? (EL)
   B: On the table. (REP INF)

React(REA) is a non-linguistic response (e.g. sitting) appropriate to a Directive.

Respond(RES) is a linguistic substitute for a React (see 6 and 7):

6 A: Open the window. (DIR)
   B: I won't. (RES)

7 A: Don't lend her it. (DIR)
   B: I already have. (RES)

Comment(COMM) is a linguistic response which may add related information (e.g. 'He asked me that too'/'Me too') or evaluate the content of a preceding utterance (e.g. 'That's great') or a related circumstance (e.g. 'It's good of you to say so').

I have already referred to the fact that some utterances are simultaneously responding and initiating. Where an Elicitation occurs in a responding slot and provides, in a tentative form, the information requested in a preceding Elicitation, it is simultaneously an informing move and an eliciting move: it is a Replying Informative and an Elicitation:

8 A: What's this? (EL)
   B: Is it a stone? (REP INF/ EL)
   A: Yes. (REP INF)

Where an exchange has two moves only, these will typically be an initiating move (Speaker A) and a responding move (Speaker B):

9 A: What are you doing? (Initiating move — EL)
   B: I'm trying to get my head out of these railings. (Responding move — REP INF)

Where Speaker B responds to an initiating Elicitation by Speaker A with a move involving more than one act, then one of these acts will typically be a Replying Informative:

10 A: What are you doing? (Initiating move — EL)
    B: That's a stupid question. (COMM) Actually, I'm trying to get my head out of these railings. (REP INF)

However, the typical pairing of initiating and responding moves depends on a second speaker accepting the lead of a first speaker and responding appropriately so as to resolve the exchange. He may not do so. He may challenge the supremacy of the first speaker by responding to an Elicitation, a Directive or an Informative with a Counter-Elicitation ($\overline{\text{EL}}$), a Counter-Directive ($\overline{\text{DIR}}$) or a Counter-Informative ($\overline{\text{INF}}$). The first speaker may then respond to the ($\overline{\text{EL}}$), ($\overline{\text{DIR}}$) or ($\overline{\text{INF}}$) directly or he may respond with a further counter-move. The following exchange (see 11) is unresolved in so far as the first Elicitation is not matched by a Replying Informative:

11 A: Where are you going? (EL)
    B: Why do you want to know? (COMM/$\overline{\text{EL}}$)
    A: Because dinner is almost ready. (REP INF)
    B: Okay. (ACK)

In addition to the possibility of counter-moves, there is also the possibility of self-resolution, that is, a speaker may himself resolve an exchange by supplying a responding move appropriate to his own initiating move:

12 A: Where's the marmalade? (EL) Oh, here it is. (REP INF)

Within a single turn, there may be several acts each of which has the same interactive function (see 13), or there may be acts which have different interactive functions and represent different types of move (see 14):

13 A: Why did you get home late? (EL) Where were you? (EL)
    What were you doing? (EL) Who were you with? (EL)
  B: Why do you want to know? (COMM/EL)
14 A: Why did you rush off? (EL — eliciting move)
  B: Because I was late. (REP INF — informing move)
    What were you doing anyway? (EL — eliciting move)

Each of the interactive acts that we have looked at so far represents a particular interactional value. The pairing of interactive acts (and, hence, of interactional values) establishes interactive semantic relations.

Conversational discourse and interactive semantic relations

The pairing of acts in conversational discourse establishes interactive semantic relations. Thus, for example, the first exchange below (example 15) has two interactive semantic relations: Elicitation — Replying Informative and Replying Informative — Acknowledge. Replying Informative is both the second member of one interactive semantic relation and the first member of another:

15 A: Where's the book?
  B: It's on the table. } EL — REP INF
  A: Thanks.   } REP INF — ACK

In example 16, there is an interactive semantic relation of Informative — Acknowledge, and in example 17, there is an interactive semantic relation of Directive — React/Acknowledge:

16 A: There's a tree over there. } INF — ACK
  B: Mm.
17 A: Sit down at once. } DIR — REA/ACK
  B: Okay (sitting).

In example 18, B's utterance has a dual interactive function: it is both a Replying Informative and an Elicitation. It therefore enters into two different interactive semantic relations in each of its interactive functions:

18 A: What's this? ⎫
    B: Is it a manuscript? ⎬ EL—REP INF
    A: Yes. ⎭ EL—REP INF

General semantic functions and their realizations

The functions which I have referred to so far are interactive ones. Each of the interactive acts (e.g. Elicitation, Informative), which realizes a particular type of interactive move (e.g. eliciting, informing), may in turn, be realized by a number of different grammatical constructions in different moods (e.g. interrogative), each of which has associated with it a general semantic function (e.g. question), and a specific illocutionary force or unitary value (e.g. suggestion).

General semantic functions (Question, Command, Statement) are determined with respect to two factors: grammatical form and communicative use. Each of the interactive acts which has been introduced is associated with a particular general semantic function. For example, each of the interactive acts which may constitute the initiating move in a conversational exchange is associated with a different general semantic function:

Only an utterance which has the semantic function, *Question*, may operate interactively as an Elicitation.
Only an utterance which has the semantic function, *Command*, may operate interactively as a Directive.
Only an utterance which has the semantic function, *Statement*, may operate interactively as an Informative.

Each of the general semantic functions outlined above may be associated with a number of different illocutions (e.g. request, order, warning, threat), and realized by a number of different types of exponent (e.g. imperative, interrogative). In terms of mood (grammatical form), each general semantic function has both *marked* and *unmarked* realizations:

The unmarked realization of a Question is an interrogative sentence.
The unmarked realization of a Command is an imperative sentence.
The unmarked realization of a Statement is a declarative sentence.

Assignment to a general semantic function depends on a combination of grammatical form and illocutionary force. Illocutionary force may be implicit or explicit. In 19 it is directly stated. In 20 it is recoverable from the content of the utterance:

19 I'll give you a piece of advice. Don't eat anything that she prepares for you. (advice)
20 I'll beat you up if you don't tell me where you hid the diamonds. (threat)

Illocutionary force may also be recoverable with reference to intonation and/or with reference to the relevant factors (including, for example, facial expression), in the general context of situation. Relevant factors in the situation might include, for example, certain aspects of the shared knowledge and experience of the discourse participants, including their awareness of the environment in which a discourse takes place and their understanding of social conventions, including those governing joke, irony, parody etc.

I referred above to the unmarked realizations of the general semantic functions of Question, Command and Statement as being, respectively, interrogative, imperative and declarative. There are also marked realizations. For example, an utterance which functions as a Question need not be framed in interrogative mood. In certain contexts, a declarative sentence will be interpretable as a Question, an interrogative sentence as a Command. Whilst the unmarked realization of a Command is an imperative (e.g. 'Wash your hands'), there are many different marked realizations. In certain contexts, each of the following may function as a Command:

Could you wash your hands?
Would you mind washing your hands?
I wonder if you might wash your hands?
You've got dirty hands.
Hands. (moodless)

As you can see, the term Command is reserved here — as are the terms Question and Statement — for general semantic functions. An utterance which has the semantic function, Command, will often be an imperative sentence. But it need not be. It may be declarative, interrogative or moodless. Furthermore, it may, but need not, have the illocutionary force — order. Utterances which have the general semantic function, Command (e.g., in certain contexts, 'Sit'/'Sit down'/'Please be seated'/'Never stand when you can sit'), may have a whole range of different illocutionary forces. Both Commands and Questions may have, for example, any of the following illocutionary forces: request, order, plea, suggestion, warning, threat etc. The illocutionary force of a statement may be promise, prediction, information, explanation, undertaking, warning, threat, excuse, insult, advice etc.

General semantic functions are relatable to interactive discourse functions, that is, they are relatable to those interactive acts (e.g. Elicitation) which were introduced at the beginning of this chapter:

> An utterance which has the semantic function, Question, has the *potential* to fulfil the interactive function, Elicitation (that is, a Question potentially requests/requires a linguistic response in the form of a Replying Informative).

> An utterance which has the semantic function, Command, has the *potential* to fulfil the interactive function, Directive.

> An utterance which has the semantic function, Statement, has the *potential* to fulfil the interactive function, Informative.

In dialogue, semantic function and interactive function are normally matched. For example, a Question will normally function interactively as an Elicitation requesting/requiring a linguistic response. However, co-text may cancel out this interactive potential. In 21, 'What are you doing' is a Question. It is not, however, an Elicitation. In 22, 'Wash your hands at once' is a Command. It is not, however, a Directive since the co-text cancels its potential to function interactively as a Directive:

21 A: What are you doing? Oh, I see. Well, stop it then.
22 A: Wash your hands at once. Oh, never mind. There isn't
     enough time.

Widdowson (1979) has pointed out that both rules of use (which are concerned with preconditions) and coherence procedures (which are concerned with determining whether certain preconditions hold in a particular instance) are relevant to the determination of the semantic value of an utterance. If an interrogative such as 'Have you washed your hands yet' or 'When are you going to wash your hands' is to be used as a Command, then certain preconditions (rules of use) such as those below (proposed by Labov 1970), must hold:

1 X needs to be done for purpose Y
2 B (the addressee) has the ability to do X
3 B ("   ") has the obligation to do X
4 A (the speaker) has the right to tell B to do X.

In each instance, the addressee will attempt to determine whether such preconditions hold (and, hence, whether the utterance is to be interpreted as a Command), with reference to what he understands to be the relevant situational factors. For example, the interrogative, 'Have you washed your hands yet' is likely to be interpreted by the addressee as a Command in the following situation: it is spoken by a parent to a child who is about to sit down to a meal, the child is aware (and is aware that the parent is also aware) that he/she has dirty hands, the child is aware that the parent disapproves of eating a meal when one's hands are dirty. Of course, intonational clues may override the need for interpretative strategies of this type (see Crombie 1985).

The interrogative 'Why don't you sit down' may be interpretable in some contexts as a Question functioning interactively as an Elicitation; in others, as a Command functioning interactively as a Directive. An appropriate response to the Elicitation 'Why don't you sit down' is a Replying Informative (e.g. 'because I don't want to'/'because the chair is broken'); an appropriate response to the Directive, 'Why don't you sit down' is a React (sitting) or a Respond.

Interactive semantic relations and general semantic relations in conversational discourse

Semantic relations involving interactional values co-occur in conversational discourse with semantic relations involving general discoursal values. A semantic relation involving general discoursal values may exist between the utterances of different speakers. Thus, in example 23, there is between A's utterance and B's utterance, an interactive semantic relation (i.e. Elicitation — Replying Informative), and a general semantic relation (i.e. General Causative: Result — Reason). The result (i.e. 'he got here late'), is presupposed in A's utterance:

23 A: Why did he get here late?
    B: He missed the bus.

Example 23 illustrates the fact that general semantic relations may span moves in a conversational exchange. Certain types of interrogative, where they have the general semantic function Question and function as Elicitations, establish a framework for a general semantic relation of a particular type between an embedded presupposition and the content of a following Replying Informative. Thus, for example, a *why* interrogative functioning in this way (e.g. 'why did he fall out of the window'/'why did he conclude that I stole it'), supplies presuppositionally a result (e.g. 'he fell out of the window'), or a conclusion (e.g. 'he concluded that I stole it'), and requests/requires semantic relational completion in the form of the reason or grounds member of a General Causative relation. Of course, because there may be, and often is, a mismatch between form and function, it is not only a *why* interrogative that may request/require semantic relational completion of this type. A *why* interrogative is the unmarked form in which a framework for Reason — Result or Grounds — Conclusion is established. Any of the following interrogatives, for example, may function in the same way:

On what basis did he conclude that?
What grounds did he have for that?
What reason did he give?
What was his reason?
How did he know that she did it?

An interrogative such as 'What was the difference between them', establishes a framework for Amplification (Term Specification). The required specification may (see example 24) take the form of a Simple Contrast relation. An interrogative such as 'In what respect/s were they similar' establishes a framework for Amplification (Term Specification) which may (see example 25), or may not (see example 26), take the form of a Simple Comparison relation:

24 A: What was the difference between them?
    B: He was successful; she wasn't.
25 A: In what respect were they similar?
    B: He was successful and so was she.
26 A: In what respect were they similar?
    B: They were similar in respect of character.

Tag questions (see example 27), cleft questions (see example 28), and cleft tag questions (see example 29), establish a framework for Statement — Affirmation or Statement — Denial. The denial may be direct or indirect (that is, it may take the form of a direct denial or of a corrective replacement):

27 A: He killed Priam didn't he?
    B: No, he didn't/
       He killed Hector/
       Yes, he did.

28 A: Was it the war that ruined him?
    B: No, it wasn't.
29 A: It wasn't Priam that he killed, was it?
    B: Yes, it was.

Inversion questions (see example 30) are different from the questions introduced so far in that they represent, in themselves, an underlying Contrastive Alternative relation:

30 Did he kill Priam?
    (i.e. He killed Priam or he didn't kill Priam. Which?)

A Replying Informative which responds to an Elicitation of the inversion question type, affirms or denies one of the underlying propositions (see example 31):

31 A: Did he kill Priam?
    B: No, he didn't/
       Yes, he did.

As in examples 32 and 33, an inversion question may actually involve explicit Contrastive Alternation:

32 Did he kill Priam or not?
33 Did he kill Priam or Hector?

There are other types of interrogative (for example, those beginning with *where* or *when*, which may request the extension of a proposition by the addition of an adverbial of place, time or manner. Interrogatives of this type do not request/require a further proposition (or propositions) bearing a general semantic relation to their presuppositions. They require addition to the presupposed proposition.

General semantic relations between moves in conversational exchanges are not established only through the framework provided by Elicitations. They are also established through the response of an addressee to relational signals and relational clues. Thus, in examples 34 and 35, speaker A provides a semantic relational signal ('if' in 34; 'because' in 35), which allows speaker B to take a conversational turn in which an appropriate semantic relational completion is supplied:

34 A: If he comes late ...
    B: you'll tell him exactly what you think of him.
35 A: He left early because ...
    B: he knew that I was coming.

The fact that certain types of construction contain clues to possible semantic relational completions also allows an addressee to take over a conversational turn and supply an appropriate semantic relational completion (see example 36):

36 A: All wild animals are dangerous but ...
   B: over-fed ones are the exception.

Of course, general semantic relations do not only occur *between* moves in a conversational exchange; they may also occur *within* a move in a conversational exchange. Thus, in example 37, there is, between A's move and B's move, the interactive semantic relation of Elicitation — Replying Informative and the general semantic relation of General Causative: Result — Reason. However, within B's move, there is the further general semantic relation of Condition — Consequence:

37 A: Why did you leave early?
   B: Because if I hadn't, my mother would have been furious.

A single turn in a conversational discourse may fulfil a single overall interactive function (e.g. Replying Informative), whilst at the same time having a number (large or small) of clauses and sentences which exhibit internal general semantic relational coherence independently of the overall interactive function. In 38, the *why* interrogative in A sets up expectations for general semantic relational completion in the form of a reason. The first clause of B fulfils this expectation by supplying the reason and the rest of the move supports this reason:

38 A: Why did you help her?
   B: Because I like her and I've got good reason to. She's always been very kind to me. For example, the very first time I met her, she lent me money and put me up for the night.

Speaker B may stop at the point indicated in 38 or he may continue. If he continues, he may develop the same topic or he may move to a different topic (e.g. what happened that night). If he changes topic, the topic change may be facilitated by a cohesive link (e.g. '... and put me up for *the night*. Actually, *that* was a *very interesting night* ...'). This phenomenon has been referred to (Sacks 1972), as *topic drift*. The speaker may eventually return to the original topic (e.g. 'Anyway, that's beside the point. The thing is that I helped her because I like her'). If he does not do so, but continues with the new topic, the addressee/s may either accept the new topic or attempt to return the conversation to the original one.

Interactive semantic relations in monologue

Just as general semantic relational coherence may be exhibited between and within moves in a dialogue, so interactive coherence may be exhibited either explicitly or implicitly in monologue. Monologue may be said to mimic the interactive structure of dialogue. Indeed, it has been claimed that 'monologue is a kind of lopsided and truncated dialogue' (Longacre 1968: Introduction). In the following extract from Major's speech in *Animal Farm* by George Orwell, explicit use is made of interactive structuring. Orwell has structured part of Major's monologue around the interactive acts Elicitation (EL) and Replying Informative (REP INF). Sometimes, Major himself provides both EL and REP INF; sometimes, Major's questions (Q) are rhetorical — they are not ELs. On these occasions, Major assumes rather than provides a response and continues the monologue as if the assumed response has been supplied:

> Why then do we continue in this miserable condition? (EL) Because nearly the whole of the produce of our labour is stolen from us by human beings. (REP INF) (Result — Reason) . . . You cows that I see before me, how many thousands of gallons of milk have you given this last year? (Q) And what has happened to that milk which should have been breeding sturdy calves? (EL) Every drop of it has gone down the throats of our enemies. (REP INF) And you hens, how many eggs have you laid this year, and how many of those eggs ever hatched into chickens? (Q) The rest have all gone to market to bring in money for Jones and his men. And you, Clover, where are those four foals that you bore, who should have been the support and pleasure of your old age? (EL) Each was sold at a year old (REP INF) — you will never see one of them again. In return for your four confinements and all your labour in the field, what have you ever had except your bare rations and a stall? (Q) . . . Is it not crystal clear, then, comrades, that all the evils of this life spring from the tyranny of human beings? (Q) . . . What then must we do? (EL) Why, work night and day, body and soul, for the overthrow of the human race. (REP INF)

Major's speech not only makes explicit use of Elicitation, it also makes explicit use of Directive:

Fix your eyes on that, comrades, throughout the short remainder of your lives! And above all, pass on this message of mine to those who come after you, so that future generations shall carry on the struggle until it is victorious.

In addition to the coherence provided by the mimicry of dialogue interaction, Major's speech also, of course, exhibits the expected cohesion and semantic relational coherence:

And, above all, pass on this message of mine to those who come after you, so that future generations shall carry on the struggle until it is victorious. (Purpose — Means and Chronological Sequence)

Our labour tills the soil, our dung fertilizes it, and yet there is not one of us that owns more than his bare skin. (Coupling and Concession — Contraexpectation)

For myself I do not grumble for I am one of the lucky ones. (General Causative: Result — Reason)

Semantic relational coherence itself mimics dialogue interaction by making assumptions about the sort of information that interactants might request if they had the opportunity to do so. The following extract from Major's monologue is followed by a hypothetical dialogue reconstruction:

And, above all, pass on this message of mine to those who come after you, so that future generations shall carry on the struggle until it is victorious.

> **Major:** And, above all, pass on this message of mine.
> **Animals:** Who to?
> **Major:** To those who come after you.
> **Animals:** Why?
> **Major:** So that future generations shall carry on the struggle until it is victorious.

Where semantic relationships span turns in a dialogue, coherence completions supplied by the second member are specifically requested/required. Where they do not span turns (that is, where they occur within a single move in a dialogue or within a monologue), the writer/speaker has to make assumptions about what information is required and which coherences should be explicitly signalled.

A writer (or public speaker) who hopes to be effective as a communicator must make judgements about his potential audi-

ence: judgements about the amount of information which he shares
with them and about the extent to which they might be sympathetic
to his point of view or susceptible to his arguments. On the basis of
such judgements, he will make interactive decisions about the
amount of information/explanation/justification which will be
necessary — about the places where, for example, reasons or
conditions or purposes should be stated or conclusions drawn: he
must anticipate likely questions and provide answers to them and
he must also anticipate the likely reactions of his audience to the
information/argument he presents. In anticipating in this way, he is
mimicking dialogue interaction. Monologue can be regarded as
potential dialogue. Sometimes the interactive component in monologue is revealed, sometimes it is concealed: it is always present. In
Areopagitica (an attack on literary censorship), Milton structures
his argument around the anticipated objections and counter-
arguments of his projected readership. He insinuates counter-
arguments into his prose and uses them as stages in the elaboration
of his own point of view:

> I deny not that it is of greatest concernment in the church and
> commonwealth to have a vigilant eye how books demean
> themselves as well as men, and thereafter to confine, imprison
> and do sharpest justice on them as malefactors. For books are not
> absolutely dead things, but do contain a potency of life in them to
> be as active as that soul whose progeny they are .... And yet, on
> the other hand, unless wariness be used, as good almost kill a
> man as kill a good book. Who kills a man kills a reasonable
> creature, God's image, but he who destroys a good book, kills
> reason itself: kills the image of God as it were in the eye. Many a
> man lives a burden to the earth, but a good book is the precious
> life-blood of a master spirit .... 'Tis true no age can restore a
> life, whereof perhaps there is no great loss; and revolutions of
> ages do not oft recover the loss of a rejected truth, for the want of
> which whole nations fare the worse.

Note

The discussion of conversational discourse in this section relies
heavily upon — but does not accord in all respects with — that of
Sinclair and Coulthard (1975), and Coulthard and Brazil (1979).
Additional source and reference materials are included in the
bibliography.

4   The functional patterning of discourse

Chapter 3 was devoted largely to a discussion of dialogue; this chapter will be concerned largely with monologue. In particular, my concern here will be with the way in which the various elements of a monologue function in relation to one another to create coherent, communicative discourse.

I have already discussed the ways in which semantic relations operate within the clause and between clauses and sentences. I shall introduce here another type of relation whose domain may extend over far larger stretches of language than those relations which have been examined so far. The relations which are introduced in this chapter will be referred to as *discourse relations*. These discourse relations are found in coherent discourses whether they be long (for example, lectures, academic papers, novels), or short (for example, memoranda, letters to newspapers, advertisements). They co-occur with semantic relations of the type we have already discussed, and it is the interrelation of the two which underlies those complex patternings of meaning which are at the core of human discourse.

Before I look in detail at discourse relations, I shall clarify the way in which I shall be using the small number of terms which are central to the discussion that follows. The term *text* is used here to refer to any uninterrupted group, whether it be large or small, of clauses and sentences which are within the domain of an overall topic. The term *discourse* is reserved for the coherent, dynamic, communicative function of a text: for text as a communicative entity. When we look at text as discourse, we look at its communicative dynamics: at the way in which its various elements function in relation to one another to communicate patterns of integrated meaning.

Although the type of analysis which will be used in this chapter is directly applicable to both written and spoken monologue, it is not usually directly applicable in unmodified form to dialogue. For this reason, this chapter is largely confined to a consideration of monologue, although there is a discussion of one dialogue.

Shreider (1974) claims that one prerequisite for understanding the way in which text functions as discourse is a certain amount of meta-information, that is, a certain amount of information about the way in which the text is encoded. In this chapter, I shall be looking at one type of such meta-information: at the meta-information that is provided by the analysis of a text into discourse elements, discourse relations and overall discourse macro-pattern. I shall also be looking at the way in which discourse elements may be linguistically signalled.

Texts are divisible into *discourse elements* in terms of the way in which their parts function to convey various types or categories of information. Each discourse element is classified in terms of the communicative function which it performs in relation to the discourse as a whole. One discourse element (e.g. Problem) combines with another discourse element (e.g. Solution) to produce a *discourse relation* (e.g. Problem — Solution). The patterning of elements in a discourse is described as the *discourse macro-pattern*. The macro-pattern of a text (that is, its overall discourse composition) is determined simply by listing, in the order in which they occur, each of its discourse elements.

The following example has four discourse elements: *Situation*, *Problem*, *Solution* and *Evaluation* of solution. It has three discourse relations: *Situation — Problem*, *Problem — Solution*, and *Solution — Evaluation*. Its overall discourse macro-pattern is: *Situation — Problem — Solution — Evaluation*.

1

DISCOURSE ELEMENTS		DISCOURSE RELATIONS
Situation	Pauling and Corey have proposed a model for the structure of D.N.A. Their model consists of three intertwined chains, with the phosphates near the fibre axis and the bases on the outside.	Situation — Problem
Problem	The problem is that their model fails to identify the forces which could hold the structure together.	Problem — Solution
Solution	We have attempted to solve this problem by proposing a radically different structure which has two helical chains each coiled around the same axis and in which the two chains are held together by the purine and pyramidine bases.	Solution — Evaluation
Evaluation	Our model has two advantages. It accounts for the structural cohesion and it suggests a possible copying mechanism for the genetic material.	

DISCOURSE MACRO-PATTERN: *Situation — Problem — Solution — Evaluation*

We can see from example 2 that general semantic relations (see Chapter 2) operate both within a single discourse element and between discourse elements:

2

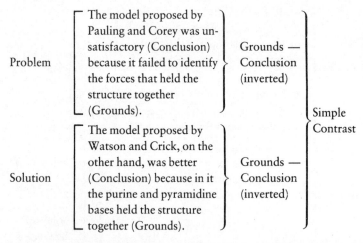

It has been argued (Winter 1977; Hoey 1979, 1983) that the discourse elements of a text (and, therefore, its macro-pattern) are not merely intuited. Although the elements of a discourse may sometimes be determined exophorically (with reference to the non-linguistic context of situation), they will normally be made explicit in the actual language used: they will be indicated explicitly in a combination of lexical and syntactic signals. If this is the case, and the evidence for its being so is extremely persuasive, then syllabus designers should take this signalling of discourse function into account. The ability both to recognize and to use such signalling is likely to be of great benefit to language students. Furthermore, discourse function signalling should be borne in mind in writing, selecting or editing materials for inclusion in language courses. In preparing edited versions of already existing texts, compilers of course materials sometimes actually remove important signals of discourse function.

Two typical discourse macro-patterns: PSn and TRI[1]

In this section, I shall outline two macro-patterns which frequently occur in expository discourse: the PSn (Problem — Solution) macro-pattern and the TRI (Topic — Restriction — Illustration) macro-pattern[2].

In the PSn macro-pattern, a problem (P) is outlined and followed by a solution, response or tentative solution (Sn). In the TRI macro-pattern, a topic (T) is outlined. This topic is narrowed down, defined or restated at a lower level of generality (R) and illustrated or exemplified (I). The first of the two texts below exhibits the PSn macro-pattern; the second exhibits the TRI macro-pattern. Semantic relations are listed on the left-hand side of the text, discourse elements on the right-hand side:

3

Concession – Contraexpectation	The worst thing about having a dinner party is cleaning up the debris afterwards.	Problem
Result — Reason	However, you don't have to worry about this particular problem any longer.	
Condition (as Directive) — Consequence	Just 'phone us at DIALAMAID and we'll send someone round to	Solution
Means — Purpose	do it for you.	

Notice that in terms of general semantic relations, the connection between the Problem and the first sentence of the Solution in example 3, is a contrastive one: Concession — Contraexpectation. Furthermore, the first sentence of the Solution is a result, the second is a reason (General Causative: Result — Reason). The first clause of the second sentence of the Solution (i.e. 'Just 'phone us at DIALAMAID'), is a condition, expressed as a Directive, and the second is a consequence (Condition — Consequence relation). Finally, the relationship between 'we'll send someone round' and 'to do it for you' is that of Means — Purpose.

4

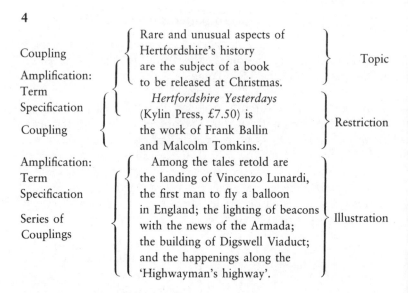

When we say that a particular macro-pattern is typical of a particular type of discourse, we mean only that the occurrence of a certain number of discourse elements in a certain order is common in that type of discourse. We do not mean that every text of a similar discourse type will necessarily have all of these elements (and no others), in that order. Thus, for example, we can say that the macro-pattern SPSnEv (Situation — Problem — Solution — Evaluation) is typical of many varieties of scientific discourse (and also of many other varieties of discourse): the occurrence of these elements in that order is common. Indeed, two of these elements — Problem and Solution — may be referred to as core elements in that they are central to the assignment of a text to a specific discourse type. Since problems and solutions (or tentative solutions) can be seen as fundamental not only to the growth of knowledge within the domain of the physical sciences, but to the growth of all knowledge[3], it is not surprising to find that Problem and Solution may be elements of discourse itself. Indeed, since much of the communicative process in general can be seen in terms of problem-solution behaviour, it is not surprising to find that Problem and Solution may constitute core elements of many different discourse genres.

Thus, P and Sn are core elements of a certain *type* of discourse: their presence or absence is definitional in the assignment of a specific text to the PSn discourse type. An expository discourse containing the elements P and Sn belongs to the *discourse genre, exposition*, and to the *discourse type, PSn.* (A discourse containing the elements S, P and Sn or S, P, Sn and Ev, for example, also belongs to the discourse type PSn because it contains the core elements Problem and Solution.)

In a similar way, a TRI text has two core elements: it must have a Topic and one other element which may be *either* Restriction *or* Illustration. Thus, a discourse may be defined in terms of its genre and its type. A discourse belonging to the *expository genre* may belong, for example, to the PSn or TRI discourse type:

Genre — Exposition

Type — PSn   TRI

However, discourses which have either a PSn core or a TRI core may have macro-patterns which differ from the typical ones of P — Sn, S — P — Sn — Ev or T — R — I and may even contain both sets of core elements. Where discourses do contain both sets of core elements, they are said to be of the *mixed type* PSn TRI:

Genre — Exposition

Type — PSn   TRI   PSnTRI

Some typical macro-patterns may be language specific or, at least, culture specific. That is, they may be typical of discourse types in one language only (though, of course, not confined wholly to texts written in that language), or they may be typical of texts written in several languages whose speakers share certain cultural traditions, but not of others[4]. Other typical macro-patterns, particularly perhaps those associated with texts dealing with scientific or technological information, may be more truly cross-linguistic. Thus, for example, it appears that the macro-pattern already referred to as typical of many texts dealing with scientific investigation (S — P — Sn — Ev), reflects a methodology which has become part of the cultural presuppositions of the scientific community at large.

In addition to the possibility of repeating discourse elements, I have noted that there is also a possibility of combining discourse types within a single text, thus creating a text of mixed type — for example PSnTRI. In the following text, the Solution is divisible into Topic and Restriction and the Evaluation also provides Illustration:

5

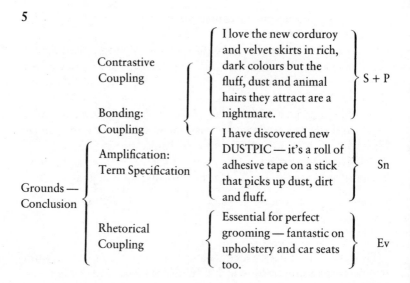

A comparison of example 3 and example 5, in terms of the interrelation between discourse macro-pattern and general semantic relations, reveals two interesting parallels. In example 3, the general semantic relation between the Problem and the first sentence of the Solution is a contrastive one — that of Concession — Contraexpectation; in example 5, the general semantic relation between the Situation and the Problem is also a contrastive one: Contrastive Coupling. In example 3, the general semantic relation between the first and second sentences of the Solution is a General Causative one: Result — Reason; in example 5, the general semantic relation between the last part of the Solution and the Evaluation is also a General Causative one: Grounds — Conclusion.

Pattern and variation in PSn, TRI and PSnTRI discourses

Specific macro-patterns may be described as variations on a theme, the theme being the core elements of a discourse macro-pattern. A text is described as being a PSn text only if it has the two core PSn discourse elements — Problem and Solution. The most basic PSn discourse type has two discourse elements only, the two core elements Problem and Solution. However, this basic macro-pattern may be varied in three ways — by *reordering*, by *addition* and by *conflation*.

Although the most typical ordering of elements in a basic PSn macro-pattern is Problem followed by Solution (P — Sn), it is perfectly possible to provide the Solution to a problem before the Problem itself has been outlined. The following PSn text has the discourse macro-pattern Sn — P:

6

Directive	– Give him a present of sweet smelling aftershave.	– Solution
Reason	– Because you want to get a little closer to him.	– Problem

As we saw in example 1, a PSn text may, in addition to the core elements P and Sn, have further discourse elements — S (Situation) and Ev (Evaluation). Although the most typical ordering, where these four elements are all present, seems to be S — P — Sn — Ev, it is quite common to vary that ordering (e.g. Sn — Ev — S — P). Further, the discourse elements in a text may occur more than once. For example, one or more subsidiary Problems ($P_2 \ldots P_n$), may arise out of a Solution and may, in turn, give rise to responses or proposed Solutions (Sn)[5].

Where discourse elements are not confined to separate grammatical units, they are said to be conflated. Thus, for example, Situation and Problem ('I'm here, doctor, because the pain got worse overnight'), or Solution and Evaluation ('I'll give you some of these really effective new pain killers'), may occur together.

The PSn macro-pattern and its signalling

It is important to note here that PSn, TRI and PSnTRI text types are not confined to discourses dealing with topics within the domain of scientific methodology, nor are they the only text types to be found within this general area of discourse. Van Dijk refers to the fact that, although scientific discourse may generally be assigned a global structure like INTRODUCTION — PROBLEM — SOLUTION — CONCLUSION — (c.f. S — P — Sn — Ev), there are also embedded structures of various kinds. He notes that 'all sorts of argumentative discourses have global categories like PREMISES and CONCLUSION, possibly with additional subcategories like WARRANT or CONDITION' (1977: 155).

Some of the research which has been carried out on discourse macro-patterning (see, for example, Longacre 1968) has not concentrated on signalling and realization and cannot, therefore, be directly applied. Nevertheless, there is available to us a reasonable amount of data which can be put to immediate use in language teaching and syllabus design. Research on PSn text types, for example, demonstrates clearly that discourse elements are almost always signalled within the text itself, that that signalling may be syntactic and/or lexical and that, where it is lexical, it is essentially evaluative in nature. Furthermore, the fact that the elements of a macro-pattern may be seen as responses to various types of question which define their discourse function, suggests a way in which we can use questions in language teaching as a guide to discourse structure (Winter 1977; Hoey 1979, 1983).

It has been argued[6] that the projection of monologue into question-and-answer dialogue form provides an important test for discourse macro-patterning. However, different questions may elicit the same answer. For example, the second sentence in 7 may be an answer to any of the following questions:

What response was there?
What solution was proposed?
Who proposed a solution?

7   We couldn't get the car's engine to run smoothly at high speeds.
John suggested that we put a bigger main jet in the carburettor.

The fact that more than one question may elicit the same response need not be seen as indicating a weakness in the dialogue projection technique for discourse element determination. What it does indicate however, is the need for more research into the relationships which hold between different types of question (Hoey 1979).

Young, Becker, and Pike (1970: 90) point out that 'problems do not exist independent of men' and that 'there are no problems floating out there in the world waiting to be discovered; there are only problems *for* someone'. If a linguistic problem need not be seen as a real world problem, then it follows that a reader/hearer must presumably identify the problems, solutions etc. of a writer/speaker precisely because they have been presented as such in the language itself. In other words, we should expect the elements of a macro-pattern to be signalled syntactically and/or lexically within the text itself. And this is exactly what we do find in most cases. Where such signalling is lexical, it is evaluative in nature. Thus, for example, 'unfortunately' and 'failed to have any significant effect' in 8, provide a negative evaluation (Ev — neg), whereas 'improving performance and comfort' in 9 below provides a positive evaluation (Ev — pos):

8 Unfortunately, putting a bigger main jet in the carburettor failed to have any significant effect.

9 Putting a bigger main jet in the carburettor had the effect of improving comfort and performance.

I shall look here at two PSn centred texts in terms of the way in which their discourse elements are signalled. Both of these texts (10 and 11) are advertisements:

10 Most deodorants are effective.
   The trouble is they don't stay effective long enough.
   As the day wears on, they wear off.
   So No. 7 have made a new extra-strength anti-perspirant that lasts longer.
   It helps keep you dry and fresh as a daisy and you don't have to worry about it wearing off too quickly.
   It doesn't.
   No. 7's new extra-strength anti-perspirant really works.
   From first to last.

In 10 most of the signalling of discourse elements is lexical and evaluative.

The *Problem* is initially identified in advance by the lexical item 'trouble' and the Problem is itself couched in terms of negative evaluation: 'they don't stay effective long enough'. Negative Evaluation is a very common signal of Problem. It may, as it does here, help to identify the only Problem element in a text or it may, as part of an otherwise positive evaluation of a Solution within a text, point the way to further subsidiary Problems. The Problem identified here is expanded in the Simple Contrast: 'as the day wears on, they wear off'.

The *Solution* is identified in 'have made', 'new' and 'extra-strength'. The Solution contains positive evaluation ('extra-strength') which may be contrasted with the negative evaluation within the Problem. The evaluation terms in which the Solution is couched become dominant in the Evaluation.

The *Evaluation* of the solution in the unspecified comparative ('that lasts longer') continues throughout the remainder of the advertisement in 'helps keep you dry and fresh as a daisy', 'you don't have to worry', 'it doesn't (wear off too quickly)', 'really works — from first to last'.

The *Situation* in 10 is the first sentence of the text. Situation is normally negatively rather than positively signalled, that is, it is lacking in the sort of specific signalling which identifies other discourse elements and it cannot, therefore, be assigned to any other discourse element. However, there is at least one positive factor which will help in the determination of Situation: some element (or elements) of Problem will make reference to an element (or elements) within the Situation. In 10, 'they' (Sentence 2) refers back to 'most deodorants', and 'don't stay effective long enough' (Sentence 2) repeats the word 'effective'. The other factors which help to determine Situation have to be taken together as clues rather than specific indicators since no one of them is alone sufficient for the identification of Situation. First, the Situation is usually (but by no means always) text initial. Secondly, Situation is often generic and is likely, therefore, to have no determiner or an indefinite determiner (e.g. *a, some, many, a few*), rather than a specific determiner (*the, this, that*). Thirdly, since 'context by its nature does not involve a moment of time unless it is a summary of events or a recap' (Hoey 1979: 41), we expect that Situation will indicate a period of time rather than a point of time. In 10, the verb in the first sentence is the copula BE in simple base form indicating a state. It is, therefore, inherently durative.

One final point should be made about tense/aspect in relation to the discourse elements in 10. It is very common for the initial clause of Solution, because it is normally presented as past with present relevance, to be in Present Perfect form (Hoey 1979).

In 10, Solution (i.e. 'No. 7 *have made* a new . . .') *is* in Present Perfect form. It is also very common for each new discourse element to have a different tense or tense/aspect combination from the previous one. In 10, *Situation* is presented in an adjectival complement structure introduced by the simple base tense form of the copula BE. The *Problem* is introduced by the simple base tense form of BE but is continued in the base tense form of 'stay' and 'wear'. The *Solution* is presented in Present Perfect form and the Evaluation begins ('*lasts* longer') and continues with base tense forms of lexical verbs.

Thus, the overall macro-pattern of 10 can be outlined as follows:

Situation (with positive evaluation)	Most deodorants are effective.
Problem (with negative evaluation)	The trouble is they don't stay effective long enough. (General Problem) As the day wears on, they wear off. (Specific Problem)

Solution (with positive evaluation)	So No. 7 have made a new extra-strength anti-perspirant
Evaluation	that lasts longer.
	It helps keeps you dry and fresh as a daisy and you don't have to worry about it wearing off too quickly.
	It doesn't.
	No. 7's new extra-strength anti-perspirant really works.
	From first to last.

The semantic relations which occur in this advertisement are outlined below:

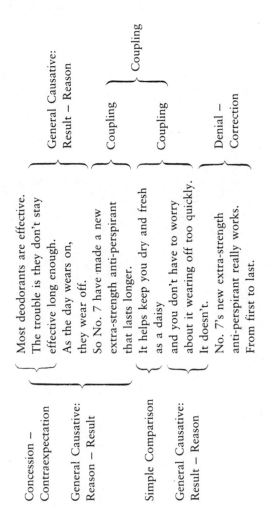

A comparison of the advertisement above with examples 3 and 5 reveals significant parallels in terms of the interrelation between macro-pattern and general semantic relations. As in example 5, there is a contrastive relationship between the Situation and the Problem. Here, as in example 3, that contrastive relationship is that of Concession — Contraexpectation. Once again here, as in examples 3 and 5, the General Causative relation plays an important linking role. In example 3, the General Causative relation links two parts of the Solution; in example 5, it links Solution and Evaluation. Here, the General Causative relation in its Result — Reason realization links Problem to Solution.

The second text, (11 below), is also an advertisement, but an advertisement of a rather different kind in that it advertises a company rather than a product. It is assumed in this advertisement that not only does the company have a problem (they wish to expand and are without sufficient capital to do so), but that potential investors also have a problem (they want outlets for their capital which are both safe and have potential for growth). The analysis of structure which follows the text is not discussed but is merely given in outline with significant signals underlined:

HIGH TECHNOLOGY U.K. COMPANY

Having developed an extremely accurate three dimensional copying system, wishes to expand and seeks capital in return for equity.
An excellent opportunity for investment in rapidly expanding industrial market. Franchises of non-technical part of the system will be offered in future. Preferential consideration will be given to holders of equity, with opportunity to convert equity to franchise capital. High earnings potential.

11

Situation (with positive evaluation)	High technology U.K. Company having developed an extremely accurate three dimensional copying system wishes to expand
Problem	and seeks capital
Suggested Solution	in return for equity.
Evaluation of Solution (from point of view of potential investor)	An excellent opportunity for investment in rapidly expanding industrial market.
New Situation (arising out of Solution to original Situation and including evaluation from point of view of potential investors)	Franchises of non-technical part of the system will be offered in future. Preferential consideration will be given to holders of equity, with an opportunity to convert equity to franchise capital. High earnings potential.

The PSn macro-pattern in dialogue

One turn in a dialogue may exhibit macro-patterning in miniature. Thus, although the overall macro-pattern of the dialogue exchange in example 12 is P (Problem), Sn (Solution), Ev (Evaluation of Sn), B's response is internally structured as follows: S, P, Sn, Ev:

12

Move	Act		
Initiation	Elicitation	A: What happened last night?	(P)
Response	Replying Informative	B: Well, we went out for a walk by the river as usual (S) but Alan got too close and fell in. He nearly drowned (P) but Linda just managed to fish him out (Sn) in time. He's fine now, thank goodness. (Ev)	(Sn)
Follow up	Acknowledge/ Comment	A: Mm, I see.	(Ev)

Very often, particularly in short, structured dialogues (see example 13), the various discourse elements of an overall macro-pattern (apart from S and P which often occur together) are confined to different moves. In 13, which is an extract from *Tuesday Call* (B.B.C. Radio 4, 9th. November, 1982), we can see this illustrated.

13

A: We're going up to Glasgow for our next question —
from Mrs Ann Crozier. (INF) Hello. (Greeting)

B: Hello. Hello. Good morning. (Greeting)

A: Would you like to ask your question? (EL)

B: Yes. (REP INF) I have a little girl who is nine months old $\rbrack$ S + P_1
now. (INF) I'd like to know how old should she be
before she starts wearing shoes (EL1) and also if you $\rbrack$
have any other tips on general foot care for babies and $\rbrack$ P_2
toddlers please. (EL2)

A: I should think Lionel's very pleased that this question's
come up. (COMM) Aren't you. (EL)

C: Yes I am. (REP INF) It's a lovely question. (COMM) Er,
the age really doesn't come into this, Mrs Crozier. It's
the stage of walking. Do not put your little girl into
shoes until she can take at least five steps unaided. Avoid
putting her in pram shoes. If you look at her when she's
lying in her pram or playing, you'll find that she's all the
time twisting and curling her toes and twisting her foot
at the ankle. This is a very important part of foot
development, and if we put her in shoes too early, we're   Sn to P_1
going to restrict that movement — and that would be
wrong. When you do find that she's able to walk five
steps unaided, this is the right time. Take her into a
shoe-fitting specialist. And you can usually tell whether
you're in the right shop. If the assistant says to you,
'What size is she', just walk out. And make sure that the
assistant measures both feet and then fits your daughter
with the appropriate shoe — which will be nice, soft,
flexible, leather-uppered soles. (REP INF) Has that
given you some help? (EL)

B: It has indeed. Yes. (REP INF) $\rbrack$ Ev of Sn

A: Yes. (ACK) And what about when they become toddlers $\rbrack$ Restatemen
and things, Lionel? (EL) $\rbrack$ of P_2

C: When they're toddling. (EL)

A: Yes, or a bit older. (REP INF)

C: Yes, erm. (ACK) Now the next (REP INF . . .) By the $\rbrack$ Sn to P_2

way, er, the next important thing is that once your daughter has been fitted properly with shoes, ask the assistant how much time, in terms of growth, does your daughter have in the shoes. (REP INF to EL1 contd.)	Return to Sn to P_1
Now, a child in her first year, or his first year, of walking will grow as much as two sizes — maybe even more — so it would mean that the shoes should be changed very often, and the experienced shoe fitter should be able to advise you how much time you've got in these shoes. (REP INF to EL2) Er, so, toddling then — I think I've covered that point, Gill. (EL)	Sn to P_2

A: Mm. (REP INF) Does that help you, Mrs Crozier? (EL)

B: It does. Yes. (REP INF) And I presume that leather shoes are — the fact that the shoes are leather, is very important, is it? (EL) — Ev of Sn to P_2 P_3

C: Oh, yes. It is. (REP INF) Leather is nice. It's kind to the foot. (Expansion of REP INF) And, erm, I know that the shoes that I'm speaking of could be considered expensive to a lot of people, (INF) but, erm, I'm going to say that, if things are tight — I'm not talking about the shoes, I'm talking about the budget — if you find things tough, then cut corners elsewhere. Never, never, cut corners when it comes to the children's feet. (DIR) — Sn to P_3 / Ev of Sn to P_1,

B: Right. (RES) That's been a big help. (COMM) — $P_2 + P_3$

A: Okay. (ACK)

B: Thank you.
A+C: Thank you, Mrs Crozier. } pre-closing exchange

B: Bye-bye.
A+C: Bye-bye. } closing exchange

It is worth noting that where turns in a dialogue are long, they may contain several different types of move. Nevertheless, whilst an addressee may respond non-verbally (by nodding etc.), or verbally (by a murmured Acknowledge), to each part of the internal structure of the turn, a verbal response at the end of the turn is generally a response to the overall interactive function of the turn. Thus, if you look again at C's first turn in 13, you will see that, although I have characterized everything from 'Er, the age . . .' to 'leather-uppered soles' as REP INF, I could, in fact, have provided a more detailed analysis of the internal structure as follows:

Er, the age doesn't really come into this, Mrs Crozier.
It's the stage of walking. (INF) Do not put your little
girl into shoes until she can take at least five steps
unaided. (DIR) Avoid putting her in pram shoes. (DIR)
If you look at her when she's lying in her pram or
playing, you'll find that she's all the time twisting and
curling her toes and twisting her foot at the ankle. (INF)
This is a very important part of foot development,
and if we put her in shoes too early, we're going to
restrict that movement — and that would be wrong. (INF)　　REP INF
When you do find that she's able to walk five
steps unaided, this is the right time. (INF) Take her
into a shoe-fitting specialist. (DIR) And you can
usually tell whether you're in the right shop. (INF) If
the assistant says to you 'What size is she', just walk
out. (DIR) And make sure that the assistant measures
both feet and fits your daughter with the appropriate
shoe (DIR) which will be nice, soft, flexible, leather-
uppered soles. (INF)

The same distinction between overall interactive force and internal interactive structure can be made elsewhere in example 13. What this indicates is that a dialogue may have an interactive macro-pattern as well as a general discoursal macro-pattern. In terms of the interactive macro-pattern of example 13, the section of C's turn that we have just examined may be characterized as REP INF (i.e. Replying Informative). In terms of the general discoursal macro-pattern of example 13, the same section of C's turn may be characterized as Sn to P1 (i.e. Solution to first problem). The interactive macro-pattern of example 13 is outlined below along-side its general discoursal macro-pattern:

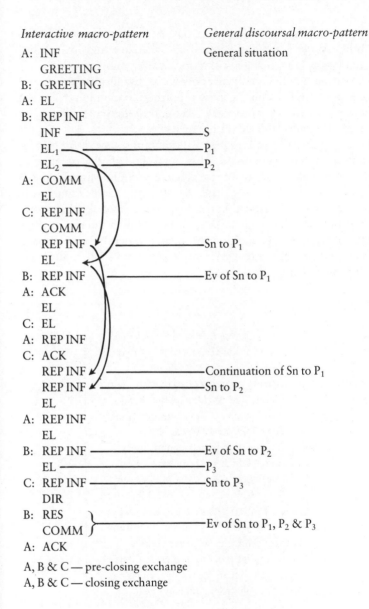

Interactive macro-pattern	General discoursal macro-pattern
A: INF	General situation
GREETING	
B: GREETING	
A: EL	
B: REP INF	
INF ———————————	S
EL₁ ———————————	P₁
EL₂ ———————————	P₂
A: COMM	
EL	
C: REP INF	
COMM	
REP INF ————————	Sn to P₁
EL	
B: REP INF ————————	Ev of Sn to P₁
A: ACK	
EL	
C: EL	
A: REP INF	
C: ACK	
REP INF ————————	Continuation of Sn to P₁
REP INF ————————	Sn to P₂
EL	
A: REP INF	
EL	
B: REP INF ————————	Ev of Sn to P₂
EL ———————————	P₃
C: REP INF ————————	Sn to P₃
DIR	
B: RES ⎱	
COMM ⎰ —————————	Ev of Sn to P₁, P₂ & P₃
A: ACK	

A, B & C — pre-closing exchange
A, B & C — closing exchange

The paragraph and PSn, TRI and PSnTRI discourses

Much of the research that has been carried out on macro-patterning in discourse has concentrated on the paragraph as a unit, rather than on texts as a whole (e.g. Becker 1965).

At first sight, it might appear that a paragraph may be defined as a unit of discourse made up of clauses and groups of clauses exhibiting general semantic relational coherence and lexical and syntactic cohesion. Such a definition would, however, be inadequate since it might equally be applied to a discourse as a whole. If we are to attempt to approach the problem of paragraph definition adequately, then we must take account of the role played by discourse elements and discourse relations.

A paragraph may, and frequently paragraphs do, exhibit macropatterning in miniature. That is, we may find that a paragraph, whilst representing one discourse element within a discourse as a whole, has its own internal discourse structure. For example, the final paragraph in 14 is, within the discourse as a whole, the second Illustration. However, this paragraph has its own internal macropattern of Sn to P_2 (i.e. Solution to second problem); P_2 (i.e. second problem which arises from first problem); S and P1 (i.e. Situation and first problem):

14

DEVON FACES Y.T.S. CASH CRISIS $\rceil$ T (S + P)

The Education Secretary has refused help to local authorities facing an education spending crisis over the Youth Training Scheme. He said they must get by until next year's rate support grant negotiations for 1984/85.   R (S + P)

P_1 A delegation from Devon County Council, which has been left with a heavy deficit because the Manpower Services Commission is not taking up all the YTS places it asked for, was told by Sir Keith Joseph on Tuesday that some other authorities seemed to be in a similar plight, but that there could be no question of relaxing the overspending penalty rules for anyone this year. I_1 of S and P

P_2

Sn_1 to P_1 and P_2 Devon will now have to decide whether it will accept the deficit, which

Ev of Sn_1 in terms of P_3 means pushing its spending further into the penalty zone, or make cuts in YTS

Sn_2 to P_1 and P_2 provision which will force it to turn

Ev of Sn_2 in terms of P_3 away some of the trainees whom the MSC is still willing to provide.

Sn to P$_2$ ⎡ Meanwhile, cash economies are being
        ⎣ undertaken at Exeter College to stave off
P$_2$ arising out ⎡ a threat of immediate staff
of S and P$_1$ ⎡ redundancies. The college has been told
           that it must eliminate a current   I$_2$ of S and P
S + P$_1$ overspending of £110,000 a year, as
           distinct from the £135,000 loss which
           the council recognizes is attributable to
        ⎣ the YTS.

However, although a paragraph may, as we have seen, exhibit macro-patterning in miniature, it by no means always does so. What more commonly characterizes the paragraph is that it constitutes a single discourse element of the text in which it occurs (e.g. Paragraph 1 — Situation; Paragraph 2 — Problem), or two or more discourse elements of that text. If you look again at example 14, you will see that the title is Topic; Paragraph 1 is Restriction; Paragraph 2 and 3 are the first Illustration (I1); Paragraph 4 is the second Illustration (I2). Furthermore, within this overall scheme, there is also a PSn macro-pattern. Paragraph 1 represents Situation and Problem in general. Paragraph 2 presents two related problems specific to Devon County Council (P1 and P2), whilst Paragraph 3 presents two possible Solutions (Sn1 and Sn2), each of which is negatively evaluated (Ev1 and Ev2), in relation to a further problem that it gives rise to. Thus, the first Illustration is presented in two paragraphs (Paragraphs 2 and 3). The first of these outlines Problem, the second outlines Solution and Evaluation of solution.

Example 15 (introduced earlier) as a TRI discourse. In it, each paragraph represents a separate discourse element:

Paragraph 1 — T (Topic); Paragraph 2 — R (Restriction); Paragraph 3 — I (Illustration)

Example 16 is a PSnTRI discourse. In it, the title is T (Topic) and the remainder is R (Restriction). Restriction is, however, divisible into S, P, Sn and Ev. The first paragraph is the Situation and the Problem; the second is the Solution; the third is the Evaluation.

15 Rare and unusual aspects of Hertfordshire's
   history are the subject of a book to be released ⎱   T
   at Christmas.   ⎰

   Hertfordshire Yesterdays (Kylin Press,
   £7.50) is the work of Frank Ballin and the late ⎱   R
   Malcolm Tomkins.   ⎰

Among the tales re-told are the landing by
Vincenzo Lunardi, the first man to fly a bal-
loon in England; the lighting of beacons with
the news of the Armada; the building of
Digswell Viaduct; and the happenings along
the 'highwayman's highway'.   I

16 *Using Computers in Manufacturing*   T

We are all becoming more and more affected
by computers. Yet, it spite of this, the general
level of understanding of the advantages and
disadvantages of computers among manufacturing managers is dangerously low.

In order to improve the situation, the Manufacturing Management Activity Group has
organized a two day seminar on 'Computers
and Manufacturing Management'. This seminar will be held at the Birmingham Metropole
Hotel from 21–22 March.

The seminar has been specially designed for
managers who are concerned with manufacturing processes and so all of the discussions
will be relevant to their needs.

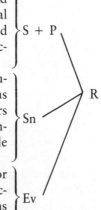

Notes

1 Although *typical* macro-patterns can be detected for various
types of discourse, there will always remain, at least in the outer
parameters, the possibility of variation and innovation, particularly, of course, in creative writing. One partial exception to this
divergence from the typical may be cases where speakers of a
particular language have a *formulaic* or *semi-formulaic* oral
tradition (which may be transferred, at least in part, to the
writing of texts), or rigid, traditional patterns for certain types of
written correspondence.

2 Becker (1965) confines the macro-patterns PSn and TRI to the
paragraph. However, in Young, Becker, and Pike (1970), they
are accorded the status of *generalized plots*.

3   From the amoeba to Einstein, the growth of knowledge is
always the same; we try to solve our problems, and to obtain,
by a process of elimination, something approaching adequacy
in our tentative solutions.

Popper, *Objective Knowledge: An Evolutionary Approach*: 261.

That the macro-pattern Situation-Problem-Solution-Evaluation should be a typical one in scientific discourse should not be surprising since it so closely parallels Karl Popper's outline of the pattern of both scientific methodology in particular and of continuous development in general. Popper (*Objective Knowledge*: 243 and elsewhere) proposes the following tetradic schema:

$$P_1 \longrightarrow TS \longrightarrow EE \longrightarrow P_2$$

Problem$_1$ Trial Solution   Error Elimination   Problem$_2$

Evaluation can be seen in terms of Popper's 'degree of corroboration' (i.e. as part of EE), which he defines as 'an evolutionary report of past performance' or as 'a concise report evaluating the state ... of the critical discussion of the theory, with respect to the way it solves its problems' (*Objective Knowledge*: 18).

4   One typical macro-pattern identified in Longacre's report (Longacre 1968) on discourse macro-patterns in Philippine languages was found in one of the languages only, others were more widely spread. At least one — a typical macro-pattern for monoclimactic narrative discourse — has since been found to be comparable to a typical discourse macro-pattern found in a number of other language communities.

5   More often than not, what appears to be a single problem is in fact a cluster of interdependent, subordinate problems, each of which must be solved before a solution to the larger one can be found.

Young, Becker, and Pike, *Rhetoric: Discovery and Change*: 93

Karl Popper, in *Objective Knowledge*: 287, expands his original four-fold schema — $P_1 \rightarrow TS \rightarrow EE \rightarrow P_2$ — (see Note 3), to the following:

$$P_1 \begin{cases} TT_a \rightarrow EE_a \rightarrow P_{2a} \\ TT_b \rightarrow EE_b \rightarrow P_{2b} \\ TT_n \rightarrow EE_n \rightarrow P_{2n} \end{cases} \quad \text{(where TT = trial theory)}$$

6   All plots can be translated directly into question-and-answer patterns. Considered from this perspective, the development of the plot seems to parallel the process of inquiry.

Young, Becker, and Pike, *Rhetoric: Discovery and Change*: 323

Monologue discourse can be seen as a kind of lopsided and truncated dialogue.

Longacre, *Discourse, Paragraph, and Sentence Structure in Selected Philippine Languages*. Volume 1: Introduction.

5   Relational syllabus design

Throughout this book I have argued that it is possible to take a discourse-centred approach not only to the problem of language teaching methodology but also to the problem of language syllabus design. I have suggested that this would involve a concentration on relational values and, in particular, on relational values of a binary type. Various types of binary relational value which exist between propositions and groups of propositions have been discussed. Chapter 2 was devoted to a consideration of general semantic relations; Chapter 3 to a consideration of interactive semantic relations; Chapter 4 to a consideration of discourse relations and macro-patterning.

General semantic relations operate not only in monologue but also *within* and *between* moves in a dialogue (see Chapter 3, fourth section). Interactive semantic relations not only operate in dialogue, they also underlie the structure of monologue (see Chapter 3, 54 ff.), which may itself be described as 'a kind of lopsided and truncated dialogue' (Longacre 1976: Introduction). Like semantic relations, discourse relations may be seen both in general and in interactive terms and, therefore, overall dialogue structure can be described both in terms of general discoursal macro-patterning and of interactive macro-patterning (see Chapter 4: 71–5). Since all of the relational types — that is, role relations, semantic relations and discourse relations — interact in the creation of all coherent discourse, any integrated treatment of discourse structure must take each of these into account.

If we are to approach language teaching and, in particular, language syllabus design, in a relationally centred way, then it is important that we should recognize that this must involve not only pragmatic considerations (that is, considerations of the *values* or *significances* of units or unit groupings within a discourse), but also grammatical, semantic and intonational considerations. Throughout Chapters 1–4, I attempted to demonstrate that any discussion of relational values must also involve a discussion of value encodings and, therefore, of morphological, syntactic and semantic structure and, furthermore, that this will lead to a discussion of generic and stylistic variation. For example, the discussion of general semantic relations in Chapter 2 involved a consideration of reference, substitution and ellipsis. A discourse-centred approach to syllabus design which concentrates on binary relational values will inevitably be an integrated one since it must, of necessity, involve all aspects of linguistic communication. There are many different ways in which a relational syllabus might be designed: there is no optimum form suitable for all language learners or all target markets. All such syllabuses will, however, have one thing in common: they will, by virtue of their concentration on language in use, reflect a consciousness of the semantic and systemic unity of the various components of the linguistic system which constitutes the target language. Any relational approach to syllabus design will be informed by the simple observation that a language is a meaning-creating *system*. Therefore, since the appropriate and comprehensive use of any system as a whole requires that attention be paid at some stage to each part of that system, a relational syllabus should reflect, in one way or another, a concern for every aspect of the linguistic system under consideration. It need not, therefore, be seen as inconsistent with the aims and objectives of a relational approach to syllabus design, that some, if not necessarily all, such syllabuses should from time to time encourage a concentration on items and units even where such a concentration involves a certain amount of abstraction, idealization and decontextualization.

The relational syllabus

The language learner and the relational syllabus

Whatever language they speak, whatever the differences between them in terms of cultural background or individual circumstance, all normal adult human beings share an ability to make some sense of the world around them through the perception of similarity and difference. They can make comparisons, they can make choices based on these comparisons, they can generalize, they can distinguish between doing things themselves (agent — action) and having things done to them (action — object). They can perceive events in terms of temporal and causal connections. This is not to say that our cultural background does not affect our perception of relationships. Members of different cultural groups will not necessarily agree that a particular event (for example, a thunderstorm) had a particular cause (e.g. the performance of a rain dance). This does not alter the fact that they share an ability to perceive, or imagine, relationships — including causal relationships between things, events and abstractions. Although there may be differences between one language and another in terms of which relational values are distinctively encoded, it would appear to be the case that, except for a few peripheral relational distinctions which may be specific to a particular language or a particular group of languages, relational values are conceptual universals.

It is a pedagogic commonplace that it is sensible in introducing learners to new knowledge or information to make as much use as possible of what is already known and understood. The new is presented as far as possible in the context of the existing. This is precisely what a relational syllabus aims to do: it aims to present a specific linguistic system in terms of the relational values which that system encodes and signals. Having already acquired his native language, a language learner has already understood implicitly a great deal about language as a meaning-creating system. He has already understood implicitly that language encodes and signals relational values and, in so far as relational values are linguistic universals reflecting connections between things, events and abstractions in time and space, he is already familiar with these relational values which will be encoded and signalled in his target language. What, of course, he is not familiar with are the particular ways in which the linguistic system which constitutes his target language encodes and signals these values.

Approaches to the design of a relational syllabus

In Chapter 1, I argued that if we wish to design a syllabus in such a way as to encourage the development of language courses which concentrate not only on linguistic units in isolation, but on related linguistic units in context, then we must find a way of constructing syllabuses which are not constituted exclusively of item and unit inventories. I suggested that a solution to this problem might be to conceive of a syllabus, at least in part, as a series of *relational frames* — that is, as a series of frameworks each of which is made up of a grouping of one pair or, normally, more than one pair of related discourse values. As an illustration of this, I outlined three different relational frames (see below) which could be constructed on the basis of a combination of two sets of binary relational values: General Causative and Condition — Consequence:

Relational Frame I

Condition → Consequence
⎨_____⎬
        Effect ←———————————————————— Cause

Relational Frame II

                    Consequence ← Condition
                    ⎨_____⎬
Cause
⎨____⎬ ————————————————————→ Effect

Relational Frame III

                    Condition → Consequence
                    ⎨_____⎬
Cause
⎨____⎬ ————————————————————→ Effect

As I pointed out in Chapter 1, the construction of relational frames such as these acutally does impose certain linguistic restrictions on course writers. This is because there are certain ways of realizing each of these pairs of relational values which are not grammatically possible where the two pairs of relational values co-occur. Nevertheless, linguistic realization restrictions of this type clearly do not provide a course writer with anything approaching sufficient guidance. Frames such as these cannot therefore constitute a syllabus. They must be modified. In Chapter 1, I suggested that modifications can be of three different types which I shall refer to as *indexation, relational cue addition* and *formal/lexical specification*. Indexation is a convenient shorthand way of imposing realization restrictions. For example, we can modify the relational frames above by indexing the General Causative relation in such a way as to specify that it should include only the Reason — Result realization of the General Causative relation. This means simply that the *cause* will be expressed as a reason and the *effect* as a result, and that the Grounds — Conclusion and Means — Result realizations of the General Causative relation will be excluded. Similarly, we can index the condition member of the Condition — Consequence relation with a label indicating that it will be a *realizable open condition*. Such a specification would, of course, limit the grammatical range available to the course writer. In order to impose further limitations on the course writer (and, therefore, give him further guidance), we can add relational cues in the form of lists of words and expressions which may signal the cited relational values. The inclusion of a word such as *because* as a relational cue imposes a grammatical specification in the form of a request that the reason member of Reason — Result should be realized as a particular type of subordinate clause. In addition to, or in place of, lexico-syntactic relational cues, we would, of course, also provide intonational cues in the form of specification of tone, key and termination (see Crombie 1985). As there are a great many different ways in which binary relational values may be signalled, the syllabus designer will be obliged to make decisions about which relational cues he will include at particular points in his syllabus. As I have already suggested (see Chapter 1), there is no reason in principle why he should not, in making such decisions, take into account the sort of criteria that have traditionally been associated with structural syllabuses. The combination of relational frames and relational cues will involve a number of implicit and explicit lexical, syntactic and semantic specifications. Should it be thought necessary to provide course writers with further guidance, further formal and lexical specifications can be included. In addition, it is perfectly possible to index the relational frames further in such a way as to indicate whether the particular co-occurrences of binary values indicated in the relational frame suggest an environment in which certain linguistic units might readily be associated with particular unitary discourse values. For example, the combination of Condition — Consequence and Result — Reason creates a framework in which the consequence/result member may readily assume the unitary discourse value *threat* or *warning* as in 'If you don't arrive by five o'clock tomorrow, you'll miss the concert because the bus leaves at ten past'/'If you do that again, I'll hit you because it hurts'. However, as I suggested in Chapter 1, this type of indexation simply ensures that unitary discourse values are not lost sight of: it does not account for them in any systematic way.

The homogeneous relational inventory and the co-operative relational inventory

It is quite possible to conceive of a relational syllabus entirely in terms of relational frames and relational cues which may, but need not, be supplemented by additional formal and lexical specifications. I shall refer to this as *the homogeneous relational inventory*.

As I shall demonstrate later in this chapter, a homogeneous relational inventory can provide all the guidance required by a course
writer, and it can do so from the very beginning of a course.
Nevertheless, it is not necessary that we should conceive of a
relational syllabus as being made up entirely of an inventory of
relational frames and cues. There is no reason why some relational
syllabuses should not be made up *in part* of labelled items and
units. I shall refer to this as *the co-operative relational inventory*. A
relational syllabus with a co-operative (or integrated) inventory will
be composed in part of structurally labelled learning units (which
focus on form), in part of semantically labelled learning units
(which focus on some aspect of meaning), and in part of relational
learning units (which focus on binary values and, hence, on
discourse construction and comprehension). In such a three-tiered
system, syntactically labelled learning units could feed into semantically labelled learning units and semantically labelled learning
units could, in turn, feed into relational learning units. Thus, the
implementation of semantically labelled learning units would
involve the grammatical expertise acquired in structurally labelled
learning units; the implementation of relational units would involve
the exploitation of the grammatical expertise acquired in structurally labelled learning units *and* the understanding acquired through
the association of a grammatical form with a particular conceptual
category (or with more than one conceptual category) which has
been the focus of attention in semantically labelled learning units.
In such co-operative inventories, the three types of syllabus component *could* initially be given equal weighting with a gradual
movement towards a preponderance of relational learning units as
courses proceed. However, although it is quite possible to do this, I
should prefer syllabuses which had a preponderance of relational
learning units from the very beginning. Nevertheless, whatever the
weighting given to the different types of syllabus component, the
core of such syllabuses must be the relational learning units. I shall
refer to these as *core learning units*. It is towards these core learning
units that the other learning units must be directed and from these
core learning units that the others must take their motivation.
Discourse must be central and those units which concentrate on
discourse values must, therefore, be treated as pivotal. It is they
that should dictate both the content of the structurally and
semantically labelled learning units and the points at which these
non-core learning units should be introduced. If we are to include
structurally and semantically labelled learning units, then we

should do so precisely because we believe that they provide us with a way of ensuring that learners will be able to benefit more fully from the relational learning units. That is, we should do so because we believe that a prior concentration on structure and structure-related meaning will provide a useful input to those relational learning units in which those structures and structure-related meanings can be put to use in the creation and comprehension of coherent discourse.

Thus far, I have referred to one type of core learning unit only: the relational unit. However, in order to ensure that the language used by learners should be as natural as possible as often as possible, it would probably be useful to think in terms of two different types of core unit — *the primary core unit* which is concerned with the introduction of new relational values and value realizations, and *the extension and integration core unit* which is concerned with the integration of newly introduced relational values and value realizations within the wider context of those relations and relational realizations introduced earlier in the course. Extension and integration core units would be concerned with more complex patternings of discourse and would lend themselves to a greater concentration on unsignalled values and on the co-occurrence of relations, that is, on situations in which different relational values (e.g. Simple Contrast and Chronological Sequence) are combined and simultaneously realized.

This would lead to a situation in which homogeneous relational inventories were two-tiered (with primary core units feeding extension and integration core units), *and co-operative relational inventories were four-tiered* (with structurally labelled units feeding semantically labelled units, semantically labelled units feeding primary core units, and primary core units feeding extension and integration core units).

Cycle and organization in the relational syllabus

A relational syllabus will be cyclic in the sense that the same relation or relational grouping will be introduced several times at different points. With each reintroduction of a relation, the focus of attention may move to different realizations and/or to different co-textual and contextual environments. Reintroduction of a relation or relational grouping allows not only for innovation but also for revision and consolidation which can take place in primary core units and in extension and integration core units.

There are a large number of factors which may affect the

organization and content of the learning units of a relational
syllabus. The factors which may impose design constraints may
relate to the need to meet certain structural or lexical requirements
imposed by various governments, commercial firms, examining
bodies etc. or they may arise directly out of the specific needs of
particular groups of learners. For example, a syllabus designer who
is preparing a syllabus for a 'homogeneous' group of learners who
share the same native language would probably wish to take
account of factors emerging from contrastive studies of the native
and target languages. These factors might, for example, suggest a
preferred order for the introduction of certain relational cues or,
indeed, a preferred order for the introduction of certain relations or
relational frames. In the case of syllabuses which are to be tailored
to the special requirements of learners who wish to use the target
language only or largely for certain specific and specifiable purposes, the purpose or purposes for which the language is required
might to some extent dictate the amount of concentration given to
particular relational values, relational co-occurrences or relational
signals. It may also suggest a preferred ordering of relations,
relational frames and relational signals.

As language courses proceed, syllabus planning becomes more
complex as the options available to the syllabus designer increase.
As learners become acquainted with a greater range of lexical items,
structures, relational values and realization signals, the range of
co-occurrence and combination of these which can be exploited in
the comprehension and construction of coherent discourses becomes greater. The syllabus designer then has available to him a
whole range of possible environments for the creation of relational
values. For example, even fairly near the beginning of a course, a
syllabus designer may wish to combine the relation of Concession
— Contraexpectation and the Means — Purpose and Reason —
Result realizations of the General Causative relation in the environment of the modal meanings *obligation*, *necessity* and *(in)ability*.
Should he wish to do so within the framework provided by a
co-operative relational inventory, he may decide to have one or two
preceding semantically labelled non-core learning units in which
the focus is on *obligation*, *necessity* and *(in)ability*, and in which the
syntactico-lexical content is made up of items and units such as
*meant/intended (someone) to do X, supposed/meant (to be) for . . .,
supposed/meant to (be doing) X, (un)intentional(ly), on purpose,
by mistake, can/can't (do) X, is/isn't able to (do) X.* He could then
make use of the content of these non-core units in a core relational

unit in which he might set up a relational frame such as the following:

Concession — Contraexpectation/Result — Reason
Means — Purpose

Within the learning unit based on such a relational frame, there might occur sequences such as the following:

He meant/intended to do X in order to (do) Y/make Y possible, but he couldn't because ...

In a co-operative inventory, decisions about the content and organization of core learning units (i.e. relationally-based learning units) should ideally take precedence over decisions about the organization and content of non-core learning units. Thus, for example, in preparation for a core unit in which *must/mustn't/ can't/could + HAVE + past participle* is to encode the conclusion member of a Grounds — Conclusion relation, a syllabus designer might decide to include a non-core syntactically labelled learning unit in which Present Perfect ± *just/already* occurs and a non-core semantically labelled learning unit in which the appropriate modal auxiliaries occur in association with the appropriate conceptual meanings and associations. Likewise, a syntactically labelled learning unit in which Present Perfect Continuous occurs might be selected to precede a core unit in which *must/mustn't/can't/could + HAVE + BEEN + present participle* is to encode the conclusion member of the Grounds — Conclusion relation. In practice, however, the requirements imposed on learners and, hence, on syllabus designers by external commissioning or examining bodies may lead to a situation in which the content and organization of learning units is to some extent externally determined. Nevertheless, such externally imposed constraints normally operate with reference to a learning block as a whole (which may in the case of state school pupils represent as much as two years' work) and they can, therefore, generally be accommodated without sacrificing too much in terms of a disturbance of the syllabus designers' preferences in relation to learning patterns.

The homogeneous relational inventory exemplified

The example below is intended to demonstrate that a homogeneous relational inventory can be used appropriately from the very beginning of a language course and can very readily accommodate the sort of lexical and syntactic specifications which might typically be imposed by educational authorities and/or examining bodies on the design of a course for beginners. The example illustrates a relational framework which might provide the syllabus input to the first learning unit of a beginners' course. Because the concentration is on the verb *to be* in its identificatory function, specification of role relations is unnecessary; because the syllabus is designed in such a way as to ensure that the initial lesson input is in dialogue form and that there should be no extended dialogue turns, the relational frame is more complex and more specific than would be expected at a later stage in the syllabus. Finally, because the intention of the syllabus designer is that there should be a concentration on unmarked realizations of certain interactive acts, the only relational cues provided are syntactic specifications for the realization of these interactive acts.

Learning Unit 1: Core Relational Unit

Theme: Identification and Recognition

Discourse Type: Dialogue

Relational Frame

$$EL - REP\ INF$$

Amplification: Term Specification (x2)

$EL_1 + EL_2 - REP\ INF\ to\ EL_2$ (Denial − Correction or Affirmation) (x2)

$EL_1 + EL_2$ (Contrastive Alternation) − REP INF to EL_1 and EL_2

DIR + (INF) − REA + (ACK) (x4)

[Order as above + continuation (order unspecified)]

Relational cues

EL and EL_1 ＝ Wh-interrogative; EL_2 ＝ Inversion interrogative
REP INF ＝ Declarative (with anaphora)
DIR ＝ Imperative (single verb)

Syntactic and Lexical Specification

Q word: *what*; Indef. art.: *a/an*; Deictics: *this/that*;
Pronoun − 3rd. pers. subj.: *it*; Verb *to be* -3rd. person (pos./neg.)
Verb − imperative: *look, listen, be quiet*
Nouns: *foot, leg, hand, arm, head, eye, nose, mouth, ear*
(Additional lexical selections as required)

Key

EL(Elicitation); REP INF(Replying Informative); DIR(Directive); REA (React); ACK(Acknowledge); x2, x4 = repeat the pattern at least twice or at least four times.

The instruction 'order as above + continuation (order unspecified)' simply means that the macro-pattern of the first part of any constructed dialogue should follow the scheme outlined in the syllabus and that any dialogue continuation should exploit the same interactive relations but need not otherwise follow a particular pattern. Whatever notation is used, a course writer is likely to have some initial difficulty in interpreting a relational syllabus simply because it will be structured in an unfamiliar way. However, as long as the conventions are explained and a few exemplificatory realizations are provided (in the form of sample learning units based on sections of the syllabus), any initial difficulties should be overcome fairly easily. There follows an example of the sort of picture dialogue which could have been constructed on the basis of the preceding syllabus outline and which might provide an introduction to the first learning unit of a beginners' course in English. This dialogue is intended merely to be illustrative. I certainly would not claim that this particular dialogue in the setting provided by the illustrations would necessarily be pedagogically effective.

The co-operative relational inventory exemplified

In this section I shall outline one way in which a four-tiered co-operative inventory might be structured. The following syllabus section, made up of the input to contiguous learning units, might be appropriate to an intermediate level rapid-progress course for adults.

(A) Input to syntactically labelled learning unit

1 (i) *Complement structure*: BE + *adjective/noun*
                        BECOME + *adjective/noun*
        Extension of nominal group structure in predicative position: m(modifier) h(head word) q(qualifier) (e.g. *very angry indeed*).
   (ii) *Used to (be)*; *didn't use to*; *never used to*
   (iii) *Vocabulary*: Personal emotion (e.g. *angry*) scaled with intensification (e.g. *angry – furious*; *angry – very angry indeed*).

2 (i) Cleft question (e.g. *Was it X who ... ?*)
        Tag question (negative/positive; positive/negative).
        Declarative with question intonation.
   (ii) Contrastive stress (with *can/can't*).

(B) Input to semantically labelled learning unit

1 (i) Durative aspect and inceptive-durative aspect (with personal emotions (e.g. anger) and intensification of these in the environment of contents of UNIT A (i) and (ii) and involving the following roles: Experiencer, Durant, Mutant[1].
   (ii) *Preference/Choice*: *prefer, rather, whether to ... or ...*
        Necessity: *must/have to*   *Possibility*: *could*
        Obligation: *should/ought to*

2 (i) *Suggestion/Instruction*
        Why don't you ... ?
        Why not ... ?
        How about ... ?
        You don't have to ... You could ...
        How about ... instead of ... ?
   (ii) *Agreement with reservation* involving the following:
        I'm afraid (that) X. { To tell (you) the truth ...
                             { In fact ...
        I suppose X, but after all ...

(C) **Input to primary core learning unit**

   Relational theme: Contrast
   Discourse type: Dialogue
   Interactive semantic relations: EL; DIR; ACK; INF; REP INF; RES; COMM
   General semantic relations: Simple Contrast; Contrastive Alternation; Concession − Contraexpectation; Statement − Denial − Correction; Statement − Affirmation/Concession − Contraexpectation; Chronological Sequence

Key:
Simp Con = Simple Contrast; Con Alt = Contrastive Alternation; Con − Contra = Concession − Contraexpectation; Aff = Affirmation; Den − Corr = Denial − Correction; Chron Seq = Chronological Sequence

bold = syntactic/lexical specification;
italics = semantic relational cue

*Sugg: environment for unitary value *suggestion*
*Instr: environment for unitary value *instruction*

1 Dialogue: any pattern of interactive relations but using language of (A) and (B) and including:

$\begin{cases}$ EL − **Cleft Q**
REP INF − **Declarative** as Den − Corr $\end{cases}$
   (e.g. Was it X who ... ?/No, it wasn't X, it was Y)

$\begin{cases}$ EL − **Tag Q**
REP INF − **Declarative** as Aff *or* Den − Corr $\end{cases}$
   (e.g. He was X, wasn't he *or* He did X, didn't he/No, he wasn't/didn't do X, he was/did Y)

$\begin{cases}$ EL − **Declarative** as Q with Con Alt (*whether to ... or ...*)
REP INF/DIR − **Declarative** (with **must; ought to; have to; should**) *Sugg $\end{cases}$
   (e.g. I don't know whether to ... or ... / You must ...)

$\begin{cases}$ EL − **Inversion Q** (with **should/ought to**)
REP INF/EL − **Declarative** as Con Alt (*instead (of)*) *Sugg $\end{cases}$
   (e.g. Should I ... ?/You don't have to ... You could ... instead of ...)

$\left\{\begin{array}{l}\text{INF} - \textbf{Declarative as Simp Con } or \textbf{ Con} - \textbf{Contra} + \textbf{Chron Seq (with}\\ \quad \textbf{\textit{can/can't; used to (be); didn't use to; never used to; BE +}}\\ \quad \textbf{\textit{adjective/noun; BECOME + adjective/noun}})\\ \text{COMM as Aff + DIR as Con Alt }(\textit{either} \ldots \textit{or} \ldots)\end{array}\right.$

$\underbrace{\hphantom{\text{COMM as Aff + DIR as Con Alt (either ... or ...)}}}$

Con − Contra (*nevertheless*) *Instr
(e.g. I used to . . . but now I . . . /I suppose that's true but nevertheless you must either . . . or . . .)

$\left\{\begin{array}{l}\text{INF} - \textbf{Declarative as Q as Con Alt }(\textit{either} \ldots \textit{or} \ldots)\\ \text{COMM/INF} - \textbf{Declarative} \text{ (with } \textit{preference} \text{ (see (B) 1 (ii))}\end{array}\right.$

It is important to note that it would not normally be necessary in a co-operative relational inventory to provide the amount of detail found in (C) above. In syllabuses written for experienced course writers, most of the detailed formal/lexical specification could simply be replaced by an instruction to make use of the lexical items and syntactic structures which occur in (A) and (B).

(D) Input to extension and integration core learning unit
   Relational theme: Contrast and Cause
   Discourse type: PSn Monologue
   General semantic relations: same as for (C) *plus*
   General Causative: Result − Reason and Grounds − Conclusion.
   Coupling and Rhetorical Coupling.
   Macro-pattern: Situation and Problem − Solution − Evaluation

Key:
   S = Situation; P = Problem; Sn = Solution; Ev = Evaluation
   Reas − Res = Reason − Result

Macropattern	*General semantic relations and relational cues*

S + P   Con − Contra/Res − Rea/Con Alt ⎫
             (although)   (because) (either . . . or) ⎬ Chron Seq
                                                        ⎭

Sn   Rhetorical Coupling ⎫
             (not only . . . but also) ⎬ Coupling
                                        ⎭
             Den − Corr/Grounds ⎭

Ev   Conclusion
   Coupling (so)
             Simp Con/Grounds − Conclusion/Con − Contra
                (so)   (although)

The relational frame in (D) above provides one possible syllabus input to an extension and integration core unit. At this point in the syllabus, a course writer would, naturally, have a great many options open to him. He could provide more than one relational frame; he could provide relational or signalling options within a single frame; he could provide lexical and/or syntactic specifications in addition to those contained in, or implied by, the relational cues. In fact, he will be limited only by two factors: the content and structure of preceding learning units within the course and the need to provide specific types of development for learners who may have particular usage requirements.

Different relational frames could be provided for (D) by integrating the semantic relations specified in (C) with any other semantic relations or relational realizations that have been introduced elsewhere in the course. For example, many different relational frames can be constructed by combining a number of the possible developments found in examples 1–11:

1 *with Reason*
   (e.g. Why not ... ? Because ...)
2 *with Condition-Consequence*
   (e.g. How about ... ? If you ... then ...)
3 *with Reason-Result and Condition-Consequence*
   (e.g. How about ... instead of ... because if (you) ... then ... ?)
4 *with Denial — Correction and Reason*
   (e.g. Why not ... ? Not because ... but because ...)
5 *with Denial — Correction, Reason — Result and Condition — Consequence*
   (e.g. Why not ... ? Not because ... but because if you ... then ...)
6 *with Purpose*
   (e.g. Why not ... ? It's for ...)
7 *with Purpose and Reason*
   (e.g. Why not ... because it's for Verb__ing (with) ?)
8 *with Purpose and Reason — Result*
   (e.g. Why not ... because it's for ... and so ... ?)
9 *with Purpose, Reason and Condition — Consequence*
   (e.g. Why not ... because it's for ... and if you ... then ... ?)
10 *with Purpose, Reason — Result and Condition — Consequence*
   (e.g. Why not ... because it's for ... and so if you ... then ... ?)

11 *with Negative Directive, Reason — Result and Condition —*
   Consequence
   (e.g. Don't . . . Why not . . . instead of . . . because if (you) . . .
   then . . . ?)

Obviously, the ways in which the theme of Contrast in UNIT C is
subsequently combined with other relational values to build up
coherent discourse will depend on the syllabus design as a whole
and upon the other items and units with which learners are familiar
at this stage. It is unlikely that all of the combinations 1–11 would
occur together in the first revision and integration core unit based
on UNIT C. Assuming, however, for the purposes of demonstra-
tion, that 1–11 have been covered, subsequent developments of
UNIT C could take the form of a number of stages in which
selections are made, as appropriate, from, for example, the following combinations (examples 12–24), using structures and vocabulary which have been previously introduced. The examples are not
sequentially ordered:

12 *with Reason*
   (e.g. Why not . . . ? Because in/by doing . . . you could/would/
   might. . .)
13 *with Condition — Consequence*
   (e.g. What if . . . instead of . . . ?)
   Do . . . instead of . . . in case . . .
   Why not . . . instead of . . . in case . . . ?
   Unless you . . . instead of . . . you might . . .
   Unless (you) X, do . . . instead of . . . in case . . .
   Provided that . . . then why not . . . instead of . . . ?)
14 *with Condition — Consequence and Reason — Result*
   (e.g. If we had . . . instead of . . . we would've/might've . . . so
   how about doing . . . instead of . . . next time ?
   How about . . . instead of . . . because if you could . . . you
   would/might . . . ?)
15 *with Denial — Correction and Reason*
   (e.g. Why not . . . ? Not because I think you should . . . but
   because . . .)
16 *with Denial — Correction, Reason — Result and Condition —*
   Consequence
   (e.g. Why not . . . ? Not because you would've . . . if you'd . . .
   but because you might . . .
   Why not . . . ? Not because he's the one who . . . but
   because . . .)

17 *with Purpose*
(e.g. Why not use ... ? It's for Verb__ing (with)
You needn't (have) ... Why not ... instead of ...?
Let's ... instead of ... so that ...
You could/Why not ... so that/in order to/so as to ...?)

18 *with Purpose and Condition—Consequence*
(e.g. If you ... instead of ... it will result in/lead to/bring about ...)

19 *with Purpose and Reason*
(e.g. Why not ... instead of ... because it's meant (to be) for ... ?)

20 *with Purpose and Reason — Result*
(e.g. Why not use ... because it's meant (to be) for ... and so ... ?)

21 *with Purpose, Reason — Result, Grounds — Conclusion and Condition — Consequence*
(e.g. Why not ... instead of ... because it's meant/supposed etc. (to be) for ... so if you ... then ... ?)

22 *with Contrastive Alternation*
(e.g. You could ... or ... instead of ...
You could ... or ... rather than ...)

23 *with Supplementary Alternation and Reason*
(e.g. You needn't ... You could ... because ...)

24 *with Concession — Contraexpectation*
(e.g. You should/could ... rather than ... because although ... nevertheless ...
Even if you ... rather than ... you might ...
Although you could ... rather than ..., nevertheless ...)

The lessons based on primary core units and extension and integration core units may involve a whole range of different procedures including, for example, role plays, comprehension exercises, the creation of dialogues, paragraphs, reports etc. for which relational cues are provided. Participation exercises may be highly controlled, involving, for example, the arrangement of a series of clauses and sentences in order to make a coherent paragraph or the placing of sentences containing relational and/or cohesive clues at the appropriate points in a text from which they have been abstracted. They may also be loosely controlled taking the form, for example, of unstructured role plays or projects and assignments. Some possible lesson developments are discussed in Chapter 6.

Syllabus design and English for specific purposes

Although it is certainly true that particular lexical items and structures may occur more frequently in some communicative situations than in others, it is equally true that, except in very few very restricted formulaic or semi-formulaic modes (such as certain official forms and instruction briefs), the range of linguistic structures which might occur in any specifiable discourse type is vast and, indeed, there are very few (if any) structures whose absence from a particular type of discourse we might predict with any confidence. As far as linguistic units are concerned, then, learners who wish to develop an adequate control of their target language — for whatever purpose — cannot afford to be over-selective for long. This does not mean, of course, that we should urge learners who wish only to be able to read and write their target language, to concentrate in any detailed way on developing an ability to reproduce the stress and intonation patterns of their target language, or that we should introduce learners who wish to use the language only for very restricted tourist purposes to aspects of the linguistic system which are unlikely to be strictly relevant to their requirements.

In most cases, the needs of language learners who wish to use the target language for specific purposes cannot be defined in formal terms but may, nevertheless, be describable (or, at least, partially describable) in functional terms. For example, the 'scientific' English relating to a particular discipline may be described as 'the realization of a type of discourse which is defined in functional terms and distinguishable from other uses of language in general in terms of what concepts and procedures are communicated' (Widdowson 1979: 27). Since there is no direct or necessary connection between functional value and formal unit, and, further, since functional values may attach to whole stretches of discourse, it is largely with functional orientation that we must be concerned in designing syllabuses for learners whose specific objectives may be defined in terms of the construction and comprehension of discourses within a specific genre and discourse type (see, in particular, Chapter 4). However, a concentration on functional values and patternings of functional values must inevitably be linked in some way to syntactico-lexical realization in the target language and, as has been argued elsewhere, this linkage may, at least initially, be established through a concentration on relational signalling. This argument is not new. Widdowson has himself suggested that where we introduce new coherence relationships within our syllabus 'these can be labelled by overt clues which are used to mark them: *for example* marking exemplification, *that is to say* marking restatement, *however* marking concession, *on the other hand* marking contrast, and so on' (1979: 257). Of course, it is quite possible to go further and to plan a relational syllabus (whether based on a homogeneous or a co-operative inventory) in such a way as to introduce structural realizations of relations gradually, the ultimate objective being a comprehensive formal coverage within a discourse motivated framework. A co-operative inventory would from this point of view be less ideal than a homogeneous one. In a co-operative inventory, the introduction of structures in syntactically labelled learning units will be motivated by a desire to provide a formal preparation for core learning units in which the structures will occur as realizations of particular discourse functions. In a homogeneous inventory, on the other hand, structures will always be linked directly to discourse functions (as function realizations), and there is no reason why the introduction of structures within a homogeneous inventory should be any less organized and controlled than it might be within a co-operative inventory. This is not to say, of course, that the introduction of structures within a homogeneous inventory need *necessarily* be strictly organized and controlled. The syllabus designer is free to decide how much control he wishes to exercise and any decision that he makes in this respect is likely to be determined in part by the age, the linguistic background and the previous experience (if any) which learners already have of the target language.

Specific relations and relational frames allow for the introduction not only of specific signalling items (which may themselves have structural and/or stylistic implications), but also for the introduction, from time to time, of specific constructions which may be typically associated with particular relations or relational combinations. Thus, for example, if we decide that a particular group of learners will be required to use their target language in the context of making and reporting deductions or drawing conclusions, we will be likely to focus on the Grounds — Conclusion relation and this will lead to the introduction of certain lexical items such as *deduce, deduction, conclude, conclusion, infer, inference, imply, implication, basis, grounds*, and certain connectives such as *so, therefore, thus, on the basis of/grounds that, given that* etc. Of course, focusing on lexical items and connectives such as these has a direct bearing on the sort of syntactic constructions that will be

introduced. Furthermore, if we are dealing with the Grounds —
Conclusion realization of the General Causative relation, it is likely
that we will wish, at some stage, to direct the attention of learners
to the meanings of certain lexico-syntactic formulations such as
must/mustn't/can't/be/have been etc.

The fact that we may sometimes be able to describe fairly clearly
in functional terms the needs of a specific group of learners will not
affect the basic principles upon which our syllabus is constructed. A
relational syllabus will be appropriate for language learners whatever their specific needs. What functional descriptions and specifications will affect however, are the specific patternings which
occur within our relational frames. In common with most other
language learners, a student of science or technology will need, for
example, to be able to define, to describe, to give and follow
instructions, to make deductions and generalizations, to state
conditions and consequences, results and reasons, purposes and
reservations. He will need to be able to provide examples, to
confirm and refute, to compare and contrast, to provide alterna-
tives, to outline problems and solutions, to evaluate, to ask and
answer questions. He will need to be able to construct reasoned
arguments, to provide justifications, to write experimental reports,
to summarize and abstract, to understand and make notes from
lectures and textbooks and academic journals. Crucially, he will
need to be able to construct and comprehend discourses in which
particular functions are combined in different ways. It is when we
look specifically at the ways in which particular functions are
typically combined in scientific discourse that we can most readily
appreciate the specific needs of science/technology students. Furthermore, where the syllabus is designed with a particular type of
learner with particular needs in mind, it is important that the
syllabus designer should either specify from time to time particular
types of syllabus implementation which would be appropriate, or
construct his core units in such a way as to suggest certain types of
implementation. For example, he might organize the input to core
learning units in such a way as to encourage course writers to
concentrate on the construction and/or comprehension of paragraph length arguments leading on to paragraph sequences (see
Widdowson 1979: 258). This can be done by constructing relational frames of specific types such as those which follow and which
might provide the syllabus input to two contiguous learning units.

Unit 1 (A)

Macro-pattern	*Semantic Relations*
Situation and Problem	Contrastive Alternation (e.g. Either A or B)

Solution

$$\text{Simple Contrast} \begin{cases} \text{Condition − Consequence/Grounds − Conclusio} \\ \text{Condition − Consequence/Grounds − Conclusio} \end{cases}$$

(e.g. If A then X so A can't be correct.
However, if B then Y so B must be correct.)

Unit 1 (B)

Macro-pattern   *Semantic Relations*

Situation and Problem (Paragraph 1)

$$\text{Simple Contrast} \begin{cases} \text{Predicate Specification (predicate = 'claims')} \\ \text{Predicate Specification (predicate = 'claims')} \end{cases}$$

(e.g. X claims that A is ... and Y claims that B is ...)

Denial   (e.g. Neither A nor B is acceptable.)

↓

$$\text{Reason/Grounds} \begin{cases} \text{Condition − Consequence} \\ \text{Condition − Consequence} \end{cases} \begin{array}{l} \text{Comparative} \\ \text{Similarity} \end{array}$$

(e.g. because if A then ... and if B then ... also)

Solution (Paragraph 2) $\{$ Conclusion   Corrective Contrast
(e.g. So neither A nor B ... Instead, C must be ...).

Unit 2 (A)

Macro-pattern	Values	Relations

Para. 1 { *Situation* — *Claim* — Predicate Specification + Denial

Problem — *Refutation* — Condition – Consequence + Correction/Conclusion ←

Para. 2 { *Solution* — *Counter-claim* — Condition – Consequence/Conclusion

Evaluation — *Justification* — Grounds ←

(e.g. X claims (that) A, but A isn't true. If A then B so, on the contrary, C must be true and C has the advantage that . . .)

Unit 2 (B) Unsignalled relations

Macro-pattern	Semantic Relations

Situation — Simple Contrast { Predicate Specification / Predicate Specification

Problem — Simple Comparison { Result – Reason / Result – Reason + Simple Contrast/Grounds

Solution — Conclusion/Denial – Correction

(e.g. X says A. Y says B. A does not account for C: it does not specify valency. B does not account for C: it does not specify valency. D specifies valency. Neither A nor B accounts for C, D accounts for C.)

The advantages of a relational syllabus

Discourse coherence depends upon the establishment of relational values and is directly linked to textual cohesion. Not only does the juxtaposition of units indicate relationship between them, so also does the presence of cohesion which may be lexical (e.g. the repetition of lexical items), or grammatical (e.g. substitution and ellipsis), or somewhere between the two (e.g. textual deictics such as 'therefore'). The presence of certain cohesive devices in a text (e.g. anaphora) may indicate in a general sense that there is some relationship between certain units of the text; the presence of others (e.g. certain textual deictics), may signal the actual relationship itself. Every aspect of the linguistic system has some role to play in the establishment of discourse coherence in general and/or in the signalling of specific types of discourse coherence. This means that a syllabus designer who wishes to focus on the presentation of the target language as coherent discourse cannot avoid taking into account the roles played by every aspect of the linguistic system. The designer of a relational syllabus will be motivated by the desire to introduce learners to their target language as a dynamic, integrated meaning-creating system. The objectives which will be related to this desire are, however, unlikely to be achieved, if he is tempted to assume that the presentation of language as coherent discourse obviates the need to concentrate on the various components which go to make up the system as a whole. Within a homogeneous relational syllabus, components of the system will always be presented in dynamic interaction with other components. It does not follow from this that the syllabus designer should feel free to assume that there is no need to control and monitor the introduction of the various components of the linguistic system within the overall discourse framework. Indeed, any decision not to do so is tantamount to a decision that there is no real need to have a syllabus at all. The great advantage of a relational syllabus is that it allows for the gradual introduction of the various components of the linguistic system within a framework in which these components are immediately put to use in the creation and understanding of coherent discourse. Primary core units allow for the gradual introduction of items and units in a reasoned way; extension and integration core units allow for consolidation and integration. Thus, a relational approach to syllabus design can have a whole range of positive advantages, among which the following seem to me to be particularly important:

1 Because lexical items of various types along with stress and intonation, reference, substitution and ellipsis all play an important role in relational value realization and signalling, a concentration on relational values creates an environment in which all aspects of the linguistic system must be treated as being equally significant.

2 A relational syllabus encourages a movement away from units in isolation and towards units in context and allows for a continual process of revision and integration and for a coherent and non-fragmented progression within the syllabus. Parts of the linguistic system to which learners have been introduced can be fed immediately into environments in which they are put to communicative use in combination with other parts of the system with which learners are already familiar.

3 A relational syllabus provides for the bringing together at one point in the syllabus of certain constructions which, although grammatically distinct, may nevertheless have the same relational value:

e.g. Being ... he ...

Because he was ..., he ...

He ... The reason was (that) he ...

4 A relational syllabus encourages an awareness of the stylistic and informational implications of grammatical and lexical choices. For example, in looking at various encodings of Reason — Result in English, we see that there are a number of different ways of emphasizing the reason member of the relation: it can, in complex sentences, be placed in initial position; it can be embedded with anaphoric reference (e.g. ... and because he did so ...); it can be placed in a separate sentence or tone group; it can receive contrastive or contradictory emphasis within a cleft sentence construction.

5 A relational syllabus need not conflict with established testing and examination procedures and is easily adapted to meet the needs of learners who require to use their target language for specific purposes or to meet the requirements, in terms, for example, of structural grading, that may be imposed by various governments, commercial firms etc.

6 It provides frameworks for the construction of useful and relevant exercises which can be easily adapted to meet the needs or interests of particular groups of learners.

Note

The roles *mutant*, *durant*, and *experiencer* may be defined (see Crombie 1985) as follows:

Account

    Mutant (Mu): the entity (± sentient) that is changed by a process:

        The butter (Mu) melted.

    Durant (Du): the entity (± sentient) that is in an identified state:

        The toy (Du) is broken.

Experiencer (E): the sentient entity directly involved in an experiential state:

        He (E) heard the music.

6 Relational syllabus implementation

I have already expressed the view (see Chapter 1) that it is probably impossible — and certainly undesirable — to attempt to separate the issue of syllabus design entirely from the issue of syllabus implementation. I have suggested that the rationale for the design of a particular type of syllabus will inevitably have implications for the implementation of that syllabus — that is, for the selection of course materials and for the methodologies used in exploiting these materials. Any decision to construct a particular type of syllabus or to organize a syllabus in a particular way must result from certain beliefs about language learning. Inevitably, therefore, the syllabus — any syllabus — will contain in its very structure certain implementational implications. I would hope that even the very limited syllabus exemplifications in Chapter 5 are sufficient to suggest to readers a number of implementational possibilities. Since all syllabuses have, to a greater or lesser extent, certain built-in implementational expectations, it seems to me that it might be a good thing if syllabus designers were to make these expectations explicit rather than implicit from time to time. In this way, they could provide greater guidance for course writers and could make a more positive contribution to language courses. This does not mean that I believe that the syllabus designer should make dictates about materials and methodologies. He should, however, be in a position to suggest that particular methodologies and, hence, particular types of course materials, might be appropriate to the implementation of at least parts of the syllabus.

Discourse patterning and language teaching

Every learner needs to develop the skills necessary for efficient selective information retrieval in his target language: he needs to develop an ability to determine the informative 'weighting' of various stretches of language in a text relative to other stretches of language. For the language learner who receives, or will receive in the future, instruction in a subject or academic discipline through the medium of a language other than his native one, the problem of selective information retrieval is particularly acute. Like the student whose native language *is* the medium of instruction, he needs to be able to develop an ability to retrieve quickly and efficiently from textbooks, lectures etc., that material which is informationally pivotal. Unlike the native speaker, he may have had little opportunity of developing the relevant strategies for this sort of retrieval. These strategies will depend partly on his ability to identify specific grammatical and lexical signals: signals of co-ordination, signals of subordination, signals of semantic relationships and signals of discourse patterning. In addition to his need to develop strategies for effective selective information retrieval, the language learner will need to develop an ability to structure his own discourse adequately, making use, where appropriate, of signalling.

The problems faced by language learners in developing competence in information processing and retrieval are compounded by the fact that native speakers may use signalling not only to lead but also to mislead. It is a common rhetorical device for speakers/ writers to use signals or cues (e.g. 'this inevitably leads to *problems*'/'one *solution* is ...'/'their *reason* was ...') in order to predispose readers/listeners to accept a particular interpretation of a piece of information rather than in the genuine belief that the interpretation imposed on the information is a valid one (see example 1):

1 In a B.M.W. you don't have to worry about ice patches, humpback bridges, hairpin bends and stray cows. Because B.M.W.s are drivers' cars.

Furthermore, cues or signals may not only be used, they may also be abused. It is not uncommon to find that the material in, for example, academic lectures is inadequately prepared and, therefore, inadequately structured. The material predicted in advance cues (e.g. 'I'm going to offer one possible solution later') may not be supplied; necessary evaluations of possible solutions to problems may be omitted. It is not surprising that students who are so frequently subjected to information presented in a way which is inadequately structured or misleadingly cued are often confused. As language teachers, our task is not only to prepare students to cope efficiently with adequately structured discourse, but to cope also with inadequately structured discourse, with discourse whose specific intention is to mislead and, most difficult of all, with

spontaneous conversation which combines all the problems referred to so far with the additional problems of false starts, changes
of direction, inappropriate responses, inattention, overlapping
and false anticipation. We can, at least, make a start by giving
discourse signalling and cueing an important place in syllabus
design and lesson planning.

As discourse patterning presents significant problems for language learners (and incidentally, in certain circumstances, for
native speakers also), it is advisable to develop methodologies
based on macro-patterning as well as methodologies based on
semantic relational texturing. Learners can, for example, be encouraged to practise writing their own material in conformity with
certain macro-pattern outlines for which a list of discourse element
signals can be provided.

Semantic relational texturing and discourse patterning can be
used in many different ways in the language classroom and their
incorporation into lesson planning is a relatively simple matter.
Learners can, for example, be encouraged to scan short texts for
signals of particular semantic relations or semantic relational
members (e.g. reasons or purposes), or for signals of discourse
elements (e.g. problems or solutions). This gives them the sort of
practice in signal recognition which helps to overcome the tendency
which most language learners have to read texts word for word
giving equal weight to all of the material presented. They can be
provided with lists of sentences or clauses — either ordered or
jumbled — and asked to link these so as to produce coherent
paragraphs or series of paragraphs. For this type of exercise, they
could initially be provided with ordered lists of relational signals
such as *and then, because, and so, the effect was, in conclusion.*
Learners could also be presented with short articles or with
abstracts of articles in which the sentences have been jumbled (see
Winter 1976), their task being to make use of explicit signals of
sequence and relationship in the construction of a coherent piece of
discourse. The following three disorganized sentences each have
explicit signalling which indicates an acceptable rearrangement:

(S1) This structure has two helical chains each coiled round the
same axis.
(S2) We wish to put forward a radically different structure for the
salt of deoxyribose nucleic acid.
(S3) Both chains follow right-handed helices, but owing to the
dyad, the sequences of the atoms in the two chains run in
opposite directions.

Most language learners have difficulty in writing coherent, structured prose. One exercise which I find particularly useful in developing this skill involves the translation of dialogue into monologue. The discussion of the relationship between monologue and dialogue in Chapter 3 provides a rationale for exercises of this type and gives some idea of how they might be approached. For language learners who have a science/technology background, it might be more appropriate to construct exercises which involve the translation of formulae, tables, graphs etc. into prose (see Widdowson 1979). Once again, it would be possible here to provide guidance in the form of ordered lists of relational signals.

It is possible to construct so many different types of exercise on the basis of relational texture and discourse patterning, that I can do little more here than provide a few suggestions. I have, however, provided in the next section a more detailed discussion of one such type of exercise which involves making use of discourse signalling in selective information retrieval.

Summarizing in relation to pattern and signal in discourse

Many aspects of discourse coherence as it relates to semantic relations and macro-patterning are particularly important in the analysis of texts in which the message is informationally dense and takes for granted a large amount of common knowledge (e.g. academic articles dealing with science and technology). Part of this common knowledge (for native speakers) is assumed to be the ability to determine the relational structure of the discourse. A very important part of the language teacher's task, a part which is particularly important where students are expected to be able to sift and assimilate complex material, must be to ensure that students have sufficient competence in signal recognition to be able to transfer their knowledge of relational interaction in their native language to the target language. In Shreider's analysis of communication (1974), there are two prerequisites for understanding a text: a certain minimum of factual information about the subject and a certain amount of meta-information, that is, knowledge about how the information in the text is encoded. My aim here is to demonstrate in outline one way in which semantic relations and discourse macro-patterning provide the sort of meta-information from which can be developed methodologies which will make non-native students more efficient in scanning, summarizing, note-taking and, indeed, in discussing, lecturing on or writing up

technical information in their target language. This will be demon-
strated here with specific reference to summarizing material
written in English. One further very important point about such
methodologies is that they can help language teachers, whose
students are interested in a discipline (e.g. chemistry or biology)
with which they are not themselves familiar in any detailed way, to
use specialist texts with more confidence in their teaching of
language.

Relational cues are normally rapidly assimilated by native
speakers, particularly by those native speakers who have an
academic training, part of the function of which is to instil rapid
assimilation of informational weighting. Relational cues are,
however, less readily assimilated by non-native speakers who are
without specific training in relational signalling in the target
language. A training in the recognition of relational signals will give
the language learner access to important cues which will enable him
to deal more quickly and confidently with complex information
and densely patterned argumentation. The lexico-syntactic signalling of relationships helps determine the informational weighting
of various stretches of a discourse, that is, it facilitates judgements
about the relative significance of various units. For example, in a
paper presenting new findings, the correction member of a Denial
— Correction relation (offering *new* information) will, in terms of
the internal *value* structure of the discourse, have more overall
informational significance than the denial member of the relation.

Where a scientific paper involves refutation and innovation, the
crucial semantic relations for the purposes of summarizing are
generally those of Denial — Correction, Reason — Result and the
generic member of the Amplification (Term Specification) relation.
The Denial — Correction relation frequently involves the replacement of a proposition whose truth or validity is being called into
question by a statement or proposition which, in the opinion of the
writer, represents a more accurate description or more justifiable
hypothesis. Denial — Correction is frequently integrated with
Reason — Result (or Grounds — Conclusion) so that, typically, we
find the sequence:

Denial — Reason/Grounds — Correction/Conclusion
or
Denial — Correction/Conclusion — Reason/Grounds

At the end of this chapter, there is a reprint (slightly amended) of
the scientific paper, published in *Nature* in 1953, in which Watson

and Crick announced their preliminary findings on the structure of D.N.A. (see Appendix). Outlined below are the stages in which a summary of this paper can be written using semantic relations and semantic relational signalling.

Students can begin by abstracting the generic members of Amplification (Term Specification) relations. These members are in each case clearly indicated by the inclusion of an indefinite determiner or by determiner omission:

(S1)   We wish to suggest *a structure* for the salt of deoxyribose nucleic acid (D.N.A.).

(S2)   This structure has *novel features* which are of considerable biological interest.

(S13) We wish to put forward *a radically different structure* for the salt of deoxyribose nucleic acid.

(S14) This structure has *two helical chains* each coiled round the same axis.

(S42) It has not escaped our notice that the specific pairing we have postulated immediately suggests *a possible copying mechanism* for the genetic material.

(*the/this* would be specific signals for more detailed reference to something already mentioned, *a*, on the other hand, introduces *new* material in a general way before specific details are given. The indefinite determiner, or determiner omission, are, therefore, indications of the generic members of the Term Specification relation)

For a more detailed abstract of material, the generic members of the Term Specification relation may be integrated with Denial — Correction and Reason — Result, giving us the following outline:

Denial	Reason	Correction
(S3)–(S6)	(S7)–(S9)	(S13) (S14)
(S10) (S11)	(S12)	
(S7b)	(S8) (S9)	(S7a)

It is important to bear in mind here that semantic relations do not occur in isolation from one another in a discourse: they interact. The second member of a Denial — Correction relation is also often the first member of a Reason — Result realization of the General Causative relation. The centrality of (S13) and (S14) in this discourse is revealed by their dense relational weighting. They form the first member of an Amplification (Term Specification) relation and also the second member of both a Denial — Correction relation and a General Causative (Reason — Result) relation. If we integrate the relations of Denial — Correction and Reason — Result into the Amplification (Term Specification) framework (i.e. (S1), (S2), (S13), (S14), and (S42)) outlined on the previous page, we are left with a summary of the article composed of (S1)–(S14) and (S42). Of course, the article by Watson and Crick, being a preliminary presentation of findings in *Nature* is already very compact. The methodology for abstracting and summarizing presented here is much more useful where students are dealing with more discursive material.

Methodologies for summarizing etc. based on semantic relational signalling can be combined with the introduction of students to macro-patterning. The text by Watson and Crick is patterned in terms of the typical macro-pattern SPSnEv introduced in Chapter 4. The pattern is as follows:

(S1) –(S5)   Situation
(S6) –(S9)   Problem
(S13)–(S37)   Solution
(S38)–(S42)   Evaluation of solution
(Sentences (10)–(12) and (43) are incidental to this macro-pattern.)

Methodologies based on semantic relations and discourse macro-patterning which involve summarizing, note-taking etc. will be related to a learner's need to develop an ability to retrieve information selectively. It is important in developing language teaching methodologies to be clear in each case about the sort of skill or skills which the various types of exercise are designed to develop or encourage. In the next section, therefore, I shall briefly discuss language teaching methodologies in the context of the development of reading, writing and listening skills.

Pattern and signal in discourse in relation to the development of reading, writing and listening skills

My aim in this section is to give a few further suggestions about the way in which semantic relations and discourse patterning can be incorporated into lesson planning in such a way as to develop the reading, writing and listening skills of students.

Listening skills

Students can be encouraged to extend their understanding and control of semantic structuring by listening to extracts from speeches and interviews or from radio and television broadcasts from the point of view of discourse patterning or, more specifically, from the point of view of particular semantic relations or members of semantic relations. They can, for example, be asked to concentrate on relations involving deductive sequence (i.e. Cause — Effect relations). They might be asked to determine whether reasons are given for the rejection of a particular point of view and its replacement by another (i.e. whether reasons occur in the environment of Denial — Correction), whether information that is signalled as *reason* (e.g. by the word *because*) can be interpreted as a genuine reason or whether, as is so often the case, the signalling of deductive sequence simply gives the appearance of logical argument. The detection of false logic is, of course, more difficult where it occurs in a foreign language.

The fact that semantic relational organization and signalling plays an important role in repartee and jokes, can be used to provide the impetus for the construction of a number of interesting lessons which help to develop focused listening skills (see Crombie 1983).

Reading skills

Students can be encouraged to scan written passages, including literary extracts, in relation to both content and discourse structure. For example, any consideration of Major's speech in George Orwell's *Animal Farm* (see Chapter 3) would be incomplete if attention were not drawn towards the conclusions that he reaches (e.g. 'remove man from the scene and the root cause of hunger and overwork is abolished for ever'), and the grounds which he gives for having reached these conclusions. Also central to this speech is the combination of Simple Contrast and Concession — Contraexpectation.

Since the recognition of relational and discourse signalling is related to the assignment of *value* structure to a text, practice in the recognition of such signals is an important part of the training in speed reading. For the development of more detailed reading skills and the more subtle appreciation of the factors involved in discourse coherence, the attention of students can be directed towards, for example, advertisements, where a very common device is the *exclusion* of semantic relational signals (see example 2) and discourse element signals, readers being encouraged to interpret clauses as being related in a particular way (e.g. Reason — Result) without the relationship being made fully explicit (and thereby possibly running into problems of advertising standards):

2 Sarah has beautiful, shining, manageable hair.
   She uses Bristows lanolin shampoo.

Writing skills

The development of signalled coherence in writing is very difficult for language learners. One way in which this skill can be developed is by asking students to prepare arguments, write down the outlines for debates, write short papers and lectures, talks etc. in conformity with a particular semantic relational and/or macro-pattern outline. This can be combined with listening skills by asking students to take notes on a short talk and then to analyse their notes in terms of the discourse structuring of the talk. Students should be able to demonstrate in their note-taking that they are responding to the clues and signals of discourse structure provided in the talk. This type of exercise is obviously of particular importance to language students who plan to undertake courses in subjects or academic disciplines where the medium of instruction will be the language being learned.

Conclusion

In writing this book, I have attempted to do two different but related things. First, I have attempted to make accessible to language teachers a number of different approaches to the analysis of discourse and to bring together various different strands of discourse analysis research in such a way as to indicate that there are connections between them, and that, taken together, they can make a significant contribution to the continuing debate on language teaching and language learning. Secondly, I have argued that the fact that the *notional* approach has failed to provide us with a genuine alternative to structural syllabuses should not lead us to suppose that there is therefore no alternative. I have tried to demonstrate that it *is* possible to construct a language syllabus which is not simply a list of labelled items and units. I have referred to such a syllabus — whether it has a homogeneous inventory or a co-operative inventory — as a relational syllabus. There is at least one sense in which a relational syllabus represents an advance on a structural syllabus: it is inherently discourse sensitive.

Appendix

Watson and Crick, 'Molecular Structure of Nucleic Acids: A Structure for Deoxyribose nucleic acid,' *Nature*, 25 April 1953.

(S1)We wish to suggest a structure for the salt of deoxyribose nucleic acid (D.N.A.). (S2)This structure has novel features which are of considerable biological interest.

(S3)A structure for nucleic acid has already been proposed by Pauling and Corey. (S4)They kindly made their manuscript available to us in advance of publication. (S5)Their model consists of three intertwined chains, with the phosphates near the fibre axis, and the bases on the outside. (S6)In our opinion this structure is unsatisfactory for two reasons: (S7)1. We believe that the material which gives the X-ray diagrams is the salt, not the free acid. (S8)Without the acidic hydrogen atoms it is not clear what forces could hold the structure together, especially as the negatively charged phosphates near the axis will repel each other. (S9)2. Some of the van der Waals distances appear to be too small.

(S10)Another three-chain structure has also been suggested by Fraser (in the press). (S11)In this model the phosphates are on the outside and the bases on the inside, linked together by hydrogen bonds. (S12)This structure as described is rather ill-defined, and for this reason we shall not comment on it. (S13)We wish to put forward a radically different structure for the salt of deoxyribose nucleic acid. (S14)This structure has two helical chains each coiled round the same axis. (S15)We have made the usual chemical assumptions, namely, that each chain consists of phosphate diester groups joining β-D-deoxyribofuranose residues with 3′,5′ linkages. (S16)The two chains (but not their bases) are related by a dyad perpendicular to the fibre axis. (S17)Both chains follow right-handed helices, but owing to the dyad the sequences of the atoms in the two chains run in opposite directions. (S18)Each chain loosely resembles Furberg's Model No. 1; that is, the bases are on the inside of the helix and the phosphates on the outside. (S19)The configuration of the sugar and the atoms near it is close to Furberg's 'standard configuration,' the sugar being roughly perpendicular to the attached base. (S20)There is a residue on each chain every 3.4A in the z-direction. (S21)We have assumed an angle of 36 between adjacent residues in the same chain, so that the structure repeats after 10 residues on each chain, that is, after 34A. (S22)The distance of a phosphorus atom from the fibre axis is 10A. (S23)As the phosphates are on the outside, cations have easy access to them. (S24)The structure is an open one, and its water content is rather high. (S25)At lower water contents we would expect the bases to tilt so that the structure could become more compact.

(S26)The novel feature of the structure is the manner in which the two chains are held together by the purine and pyramidine bases. (S27)The planes of the bases are perpendicular to the fibre axis. (S28)They are joined together in pairs, a single base from one chain being hydrogen-bonded to a single base from the other chain, so that the two lie side by side with identical z-co-ordinates. (S29)One of the pairs must be a purine and the other a pyramidine for bonding to occur. (S30) The hydrogen bonds are made as follows: purine position 1 to pyramidine position 1; purine position 6 to pyramidine position 6.

(S31)If it is assumed that the bases only occur in the structure in the most plausible tautomeric forms (that is, with the keto rather than the enol configurations) it is found that only specific pairs of bases can bond together. (S32)These pairs are: adenine (purine) with thymine (pyramidine), and guanine (purine) with cytosine (pyramidine).

(S33)In other words, if an adenine forms one member of a pair, on either chain, then on these assumptions the other member must be thymine; similarly for guanine and cytosine. (S34)The sequence of bases on a single chain does not appear to be restricted in any way. (S35)However, if only specific pairs of bases can be formed, it follows that if the sequence of bases on one chain is given, then the sequence on the other chain is automatically determined.

(S36)It has been found experimentally that the ratio of the amounts of adenine to thymine, and the ratio of guanine to cytosine, are always very close to unity for deoxyribose nucleic acid. (S37)It is probably impossible to build this structure with a ribose sugar in place of the deoxyribose, as the extra oxygen atom would make too close a van der Waals contact.

(S38)The previously published X-ray data on deoxyribose nucleic acid are insufficient for a rigorous test of our structure. (S39)So far as we can tell, it is roughly compatible with the experimental data, but it must be regarded as unproved until it has been checked against more exact results. (S40)Some of these are given in the following communications. (S41)We were not aware of the details of the results presented there when we devised our structure, which rests mainly though not entirely on published experimental data and stereo-chemical arguments. (S42)It has not escaped our notice that the specific pairing we have postulated immediately suggests a possible copying mechanism for the genetic material. (S 43)Full details of the structure, including the conditions assumed in building it, together with a set of co-ordinates for the atoms, will be published elsewhere.

(The example text above has been slightly amended by omission.)

Bibliography

Anderson, J. M. 1971. *The grammar of case: Towards a localistic theory*. Cambridge: Cambridge University Press.

Atlas, J. D. and **S. Levinson** 1981. 'It-clefts, informativeness and logical form: radical pragmatics (revised standard version)'. In Cole 1981: 1–61.

Austin, J. L. 1962. *How To Do Things With Words*. Oxford: Clarendon Press.

Bach, E. and **R. T. Harms** (eds.) 1970. *Universals in Linguistic Theory*. London: Holt, Rinehart & Winston.

Bach, K. and **R. M. Harnish** 1979. *Linguistic Communication and Speech Acts*. Cambridge, Mass.: MIT Press.

Ballard, D. L., R. J. Conrad, and **R. E. Longacre** 1974. 'The Deep and Surface Grammar of Interclausal Relations'. In Brend 1974: 307–55.

Bauman, R. and **J. Sherzer** (eds.) 1974. *Explorations in the Ethnography of Speaking*. Cambridge: Cambridge University Press.

Beaugrande, R. de and **W. Dressler** 1981. *Introduction to Text Linguistics*. London: Longman.

Becker, A. L. 1965. 'A Tagmemic Approach to Paragraph Analysis'. *College Composition and Communication* 16: 237–42.

Becker, A. L. 1966. 'Symposium on the Paragraph'. *College Composition and Communication* 17: 67–72.

Becker, A. L. 1974. 'Conjoining in a Tagmemic Grammar of English'. In Brend 1974: 223–33.

Beekman, J. and **J. Callow** 1974. *Translating the Word of God*. Michigan: Zondervan.

Bell, R. T. 1981. *An Introduction to Applied Linguistics: Approaches and Methods in Language Teaching*. London: Batsford.

Bennett, M. and **B. Partee** 1978. *Toward the Logic of Tense and Aspect in English*. Bloomington, Indiana: Indiana University Linguistics Club.

Berry, M. 1981. 'Systemic Linguistics and Discourse Analysis'. In Coulthard and Montgomery 1981: 120–45.

Bolinger, D. 1982. 'Intonation and Its Parts'. *Language* 58: 505–29.

Brazil, D. C. 1975. 'Discourse Intonation'. *Discourse Analysis Monographs* no. 1, University of Birmingham, English Language Research.

Brazil, D. C., R. M. Coulthard , and C. M. Johns 1980. *Discourse Intonation and Language Teaching*. London: Longman.

Brend, R. M. (ed.) 1974. *Advances in Tagmemics*. New York: North Holland.

British Council. 1979–80. *Reading and Thinking in English*. Oxford: Oxford University Press.

Brown, G. and G. Yule 1983. *Discourse Analysis*. Cambridge: Cambridge University Press.

Brown, P. and S. Levinson 1978. 'Universals in language usage: politeness phenomena'. In E. Goody 1978: 56–311.

Brumfit, C. J. and K. Johnson (eds.) 1979. *The Communicative Approach to Language Teaching*. Oxford: Oxford University Press.

Burton, D. 1981. 'Analysing Spoken Discourse'. In Coulthard and Montgomery 1981: 61–81.

Burton, D. 1982. 'Conversation Pieces'. In Carter and Burton 1982: 86–111.

Carter, R. and D. Burton (eds.) 1982. *Literary Text and Language Study*. London: Edward Arnold.

Chafe, W. L. 1970. *Meaning and the Structure of Language*. Chicago: The University of Chicago Press.

Chandler, R. 1944. *The Lady in The Lake*. London: Hamish Hamilton.

Chandler, R. 1949. *Farewell, My Lovely*. Harmondsworth: Penguin.

Chandler, R. 1953. *The Long Good-Bye*. London: Hamish Hamilton.

Chandler, R. 1958. *Playback*. London: Hamish Hamilton.

Cole, P. (ed.) 1978. *Syntax and Semantics, 9: Pragmatics*. New York: Academic Press.

Cole, P. (ed.) 1981. *Radical Pragmatics*. New York: Academic Press.

Cole, P. and J. L. Morgan (eds.) 1975. *Syntax and Semantics, 3: Speech Acts*. New York: Academic Press.

Cook, W. A. 1979. *Case Grammar: Development of the Matrix Model*. Washington, D.C.: Georgetown University Press.

Copeland, J. E. and P. W. Davis (eds.) 1981. *Seventh Lacus Forum 1980*. Columbia: Hornbeam.

Corder, S. P. and E. Roulet (eds.) 1974. *Linguistic Insights in Applied Linguistics*. Brussels: AIMAV. Paris: Didier.

Coulthard, R. M. 1975. 'Discourse Analysis in English: a review of the literature'. *Language and Linguistics Abstracts* 8: 1.

Coulthard, R. M. 1977. *An Introduction to Discourse Analysis*. London: Longman.

Coulthard, R. M. and D. C. Brazil 1979. 'Exchange Structure'. *Discourse Analysis Monographs* no. 5, University of Birmingham, English Language Research.

Coulthard, M. and M. Montgomery (eds.) 1981. *Studies in Discourse Analysis*. London: Routledge & Kegan Paul.

Crombie, W. 1982. 'The application of some recent research in Text Semantics to the teaching of English as a foreign language', *The British Journal of Language Teaching* 20: 47–51.

Crombie, W. 1983. 'Raymond Chandler: Burlesque, Parody, Paradox', *Language and Style* 16: 151–67.

Crombie, W. 1985. *Process and Relation in Discourse and Language Learning*. Oxford: Oxford University Press.

Dea (Crombie), W. and N. J. Belkin 1978. 'Beyond the sentence: clause relations and textual analysis'. *Informatics* 3 (Aslib): 67–84.

Dillon, G. L. 1977. *Introduction to Contemporary Linguistic Semantics*. New Jersey: Prentice-Hall.

Edmondson, W. 1981. *Spoken Discourse: a model for analysis*. London: Longman.

Fillmore, C. J. 1968; rpt. 1972. 'The Case for Case'. In Bach and Harms 1968; rpt. 1972: 1–88.

Fillmore, C. J. 1975. *Santa Cruz Lectures on Deixis 1971*. Mimeo, Indiana University Linguistics Club.

Frantz, D. G. 1970. *Toward a Generative Grammar of Blackfoot*. University of Alberta PhD dissertation, reissued in Summer Institute of Linguistics Publications in Linguistics.

Fuller, D. P. 1959. *The Inductive Method of Bible Study*, 3rd. ed. Pasadena: Fuller Theological Seminary, mimeo.

Gazdar, G., **Pullum,** and **I.** Sag 1981. *Auxiliaries and Related Phenomena In a Restrictive Theory of Grammar.* Indiana: Indiana University Linguistics Club.

Givon, T. (ed.) 1979. *Syntax and Semantics: Vol. 12: Discourse and Syntax.* New York: Academic Press.

Goody, E. (ed.) 1978. *Questions and Politeness: Strategies in Social Interaction.* Cambridge: Cambridge University Press.

Gorayska, B. 1978–79. 'The English Verb System'. *Interlanguage Studies Bulletin:* Utrecht, 1978, 3: 234–249 and 1979, 4: 114–32.

Graustein, G. W. T. 1981. 'Principles of text analysis', *Linguistische Arbeitsberichte* 31: 3–37.

Greenberg, J. H. (ed.) 1963 *Universals of Language.* Massachusetts: Massachusetts Institute of Technology.

Grice, H. P. 1968. 'Utterer's meaning, sentence-meaning, and word-meaning', *Foundations of Language* 4: 1–18.

Grice, H. P. 1975. 'Logic and conversation'. In Cole and Morgan 1975: 41–58.

Grice, H. P. 1978. 'Further notes on logic and conversation'. In Cole and Morgan 1978: 113–28.

Grice, H. P. 1981. 'Presupposition and conversational implicature'. In Cole 1981: 183–98.

Grimes, J. E. 1975. *The Thread of Discourse.* The Hague: Mouton.

Gumperz, J. J. and **D. H. Hymes** (eds.) 1972. *Directions in Sociolinguistics.* New York: Holt, Rinehart & Winston.

Halliday, M. A. K. 1961. 'Categories of the Theory of Grammar'. *Word,* 17, 241–92.

Halliday, M. A. K. 1970a. *A Course in Spoken English: Intonation.* London: Oxford University Press.

Halliday, M. A. K. 1970b. 'Functional Diversity in Language as seen from a Consideration of Modality and Mood in English'. *Foundations of Language* 6: 322–61.

Halliday, M. A. K. 1973. *Explorations in the Functions of Language.* London: Edward Arnold.

Halliday, M. A. K. 1975. *Learning How To Mean: Explorations in the Development of Language.* London: Edward Arnold.

Halliday, M. A. K. 1981. 'Text Semantics and Clause Grammar: some patterns of realization'. In Copeland and Davis 1981: 31–60.

Halliday, M. A. K. and **R. Hasan** 1976. *Cohesion in English.* London: Longman.

Heinämäki, O. 1978. *Semantics of English Temporal Connectives.* Indiana: Indiana University Linguistics Club.

Hoey, M. 1979. 'Signalling in Discourse'. *Discourse Analysis Monographs* no. 6, University of Birmingham, English Language Research.

Hoey, M. 1983. *On the Surface of Discourse.* London: George Allen & Unwin.

Jakobson, J. H. 1963. 'Some Universals of Grammar with Particular Reference to the Order of the Meaningful Elements'. In Greenberg 1963, 2nd. ed. 1966: 73–113.

Koen, F. A., L. Becker, and **R. Young** 1969. 'The Psychological Reality of the Paragraph': *Journal of Verbal Learning and Verbal Behaviour* 8: 49–53.

Kress, G. (ed.) 1976. *Halliday: System and Function in Language: selected papers.* London: Oxford University Press.

Labov, W. 1970. 'The Study of Language in its Social Context'. *Studium Generale.* Vol. 23, reprinted in Labov 1972a.

Labov, W. 1972a. *Sociolinguistic Patterns.* Philadelphia: University of Pennsylvania Press.

Labov, W. 1972b. 'Rules for ritual insults'. In Sudnow 1972: 120–69.

Lakoff, R. 1972. 'Language in Context', *Language* 48: 907–27.

Leech, G. N. 1980. *Explorations in Semantics and Pragmatics.* Amsterdam: John Benjamins.

Leech, G. N. 1983. *Principles of Pragmatics.* London: Longman.

Leech, G. N. and **J. Svartvik** 1975. *A Communicative Grammar of English.* London: Longman.

Levinson, S. C. 1979a. 'Activity types and language'. *Linguistics* 17: 356–99.

Levinson, S. C. 1979b. 'Pragmatics and social deixis'. *Proceedings of the Fifth Annual Meeting of the Berkley Linguistic Society.* 1979: 206–23.

Levinson, S. C. 1983. *Pragmatics.* Cambridge: Cambridge University Press.

Longacre, R. E. 1968. *Discourse, Paragraph and Sentence Structure in Selected Philippine Languages.* Vol. 1: *Discourse and Paragraph Structure.* Santa Ana, California: Summer Institute of Linguistics.

Longacre, R. E. 1970a. 'Sentence Structure as a Statement Calculus' *Language* 46: 783–815.

Longacre, R. E. 1970b. 'The paragraph as a grammatical unit'. In Givon 1979.

Longacre, R. E. 1972. *Hierarchy and Universality of Discourse Constituents in New Guinea Languages: Discussion*. Washington, D.C.: Georgetown University Press.

Longacre, R. E. 1974. 'Narrative Versus Other Discourse Genre'. In Brend 1974: 357–75.

Longacre, R. E. 1976. *An Anatomy of Speech Notions*. Lisse: Peter de Ridder.

Lyons, J. 1968. *Introduction to Theoretical Linguistics*. Cambridge: Cambridge University Press.

Lyons, J. 1977. *Semantics*. Vols. 1 and 2. Cambridge: Cambridge University Press.

Lyons, J. 1981. *Language, Meaning and Context*. London: Fontana.

Monaghan, J. 1979. *The Neo-Firthian Tradition and its Contribution to General Linguistics*. Tübingen, W. Germany: Niemeyer.

Munby, J. 1978. *Communicative Syllabus Design*. Cambridge: Cambridge University Press.

O'Brien, R. J. (ed.) 1971. *Georgetown University Round Table on Languages and Linguistics 1971*. Washington, D.C.: Georgetown University Press.

Orwell, G. 1951. *Animal Farm: A Fairy Story*. Harmondsworth: Penguin.

Oster, S. 1981. 'The Use of Tenses in "Reporting Past Literature" in EST'. In Selinker *et al.* 1981: 76–90.

Palmer, F. R. 1979. *Modality and the English Modals*. London: Longman.

Parret. H., M. Sbisà, and J. Verschueren (eds.) 1981. *Possibilities and Limitations of Pragmatics: Proceedings of the Conference on Pragmatics at Urbino, July 8–14, 1979*. Amsterdam: Benjamins.

Patrides, C. A. (ed.) 1974. *John Milton: Selected Prose*. Penguin English Library. Harmondsworth: Penguin.

Pike, K. L. 1966. *Tagmemic and Matrix Linguistics Applied to Selected African Languages*. U.S. Dept. of Health, Education and Welfare, Office of Education, Bureau of Research.

Popper, K. R. 1972. *Objective Knowledge: An Evolutionary Approach*. Oxford: Oxford University Press.

Quirk, R., S. Greenbaum, G. N. Leech and J. Svartvik 1972. *A Grammar of Contemporary English*. London: Longman.

Richardson, K. 1981. 'Sentences in Discourse'. In Coulthard and Montgomery 1981: 51–60.

Sacks, H. 1972. 'On the Analyzability of Stories by Children'. In Gumperz and Hymes 1972: 325–45.

Sacks, H., E. Schegloff, and G. Jefferson 1974. 'A Simplest Systematics for the Analysis of Turn Taking in Conversation'. *Language* 50: 696–735.

Saussure, F. de. 1916, trans. 1959. *Course in General Linguistics*, transl. Wade Baskin. New York: Philosophical Library.

Schegloff, E. and H. Sacks 1973. 'Opening Up Closings'. *Semiotica* 8: 289–327.

Schmidt, M. F. 1981. 'Needs Assessment in English for Specific Purposes: The Case Study'. In Selinker *et al.* 1981: 199–210.

Searle, J. R. 1969. *Speech Acts: An Essay on the Philosophy of Language*. Cambridge: Cambridge University Press.

Searle, J. R. (ed.) 1971. *The Philosophy of Language*. Oxford: Oxford University Press.

Selinker, L., E. Tarone, and V. H. Hanzeli 1981. *English for Academic and Technical Purposes*. Massachusetts: Newbury House.

Shreider, IU. A. 1974. 'Informatsiia i metainformatsiia', *Nauchno-Tekhnicheskaia Informatsiia*, Seria 2, No. 4: 3–10.

Sinclair, J. McH. and R. M. Coulthard 1975. *Towards an Analysis of Discourse: The English used by teachers and pupils*. London: Oxford University Press.

Stubbs, M. 1983. *Discourse Analysis: The Sociolinguistic Analysis of Natural Language*. Oxford: Basil Blackwell.

Sudnow, D. (ed.) 1972. *Studies in Social Interaction*. New York: Free Press.

Titone, R. 1968. *Teaching Foreign Languages: A Historical Sketch*. Georgetown: Georgetown University Press.

Trim, J.M.L., R. Richterich, J. A. Van Ek, and D. A. Wilkins 1980. *Systems Development in Adult Language Learning*. (Council of Europe Modern Languages Project). Oxford: Pergamon.

Turner, R. (ed.) 1974. *Ethnomethodology: Selected Readings.* Harmondsworth: Penguin Education.

Van der Auwera, J. 1980. *Indirect Speech Acts Revisited.* Indiana: Indiana University Linguistics Club.

Van Dijk, T. A. 1972. *Some Aspects of Text Grammars.* The Hague: Mouton.

Van Dijk, T. A. 1976. *Pragmatics of Language and Literature.* Amsterdam: North Holland.

Van Dijk, T. A. 1977. *Text and Context: Explorations in the Semantics and Pragmatics of Discourse.* London: Longman.

Van Ek, J. A. 1975. *The Threshold Level.* Strasbourg: Council of Europe.

Van Ek, J. A. and **L. G. Alexander** 1977. *Waystage: Systems Development in Adult Language Learning.* Strasbourg: Council of Europe.

Verdoodt, A. (ed.) 1974. *Proceedings of the Third International Congress of Applied Linguistics: Vol. 2.* Heidelberg: Julius Groos.

Widdowson, H. G. 1972. 'The teaching of English as communication'. *English Language Teaching Journal* 27: 15–19.

Widdowson, H. G. 1978. *Teaching Language as Communication.* Oxford: Oxford University Press.

Widdowson, H. G. 1979. *Explorations in Applied Linguistics.* Oxford: Oxford University Press.

Widdowson, H. G. 1981. 'English for Specific Purposes: Criteria for Course Design'. In Selinker *et al.* 1981: 1–11.

Wilkins, D. A. 1972a. 'An investigation into the linguistic and situational common core in a unit of the credit system'. Strasbourg: Council of Europe.

Wilkins, D. A. 1972b. 'Grammatical, Situational and Notional Syllabuses'. In Brumfit and Johnson 1979: 82–90.

Wilkins, D. A. 1973. 'The linguistic and situational content of the common core in a unit/credit system'. In Trim *et al.* 1973: 129–46.

Wilkins, D. A. 1974. 'Notional Syllabuses and the Concept of a Minimum Adequate Grammar'. In Brumfit and Johnson 1979: 91–98. Also in Corder and Roulet: 1974.

Wilkins, D. A. 1976. *Notional Syllabuses.* London: Oxford University Press.

Wilson, D. 1975. *Presuppositions and Non-Truth Conditional Semantics*. New York: Academic Press.

Winter, E. O. 1974. 'Replacement as a function of repetition: a study of its principal features in the clause relations of contemporary English'. PhD Thesis, University of London.

Winter, E. O. 1976. 'Fundamentals of Information Science'. Hatfield: The Hatfield Polytechnic.

Winter, E. O. 1977. 'A Clause-Relational Approach to English Texts: A Study of Some Predictive Lexical Items in Written Discourse'. *Instructional Science* 6: 1 (special issue).

Winter, E. O. 1982. *Towards a Contextual Grammar of English*. London: George Allen & Unwin.

Wittgenstein, L. 1958. *Philosophical Investigations*. Oxford: Basil Blackwell.

Young, R. and **A. Becker** 1966. 'The role of lexical and grammatical clues in paragraph recognition'. In *Studies in Language and Language Behavior*, Progress Report No. 2. Ann Arbor, Michigan: Center for Research on Language, University of Michigan.

Young, R., A. Becker, and **K. Pike** 1970. *Rhetoric: Discovery and Change*. New York: Harcourt, Brace & World.